"We are story people, created by a storytelling God. *Get Your Story Straight* is a brilliant resource designed to help students discover the beauty and power of the greatest story ever written, the story of Jesus. This guide provides a creative and clear way for students to unpack the living and breathing Word of God."

Louie Giglio, Passion City Church/Passion Conferences

"If you're a teenager, you should know some things about Kristen Hatton and her new book: 1) She'll speak to you honestly; there's no soft-peddling the big issues. 2) She'll treat you with dignity; there's no talking down here. 3) She'll take you seriously; she knows what's at stake in your life. 4) She'll help you to maturity; she's learned the path. Good reasons to make *Get Your Story Straight* your book of the year!"

Sinclair B. Ferguson, Professor of Systematic Theology, Redeemer Seminary, Dallas

"After working with teenagers for decades, I am well aware of the challenges that come with adolescence. Kristen Hatton cuts to the heart of today's 'me-centered' culture by placing Christ as the true hero of everyone's story. With a heavy emphasis on how God exists for his own glory, this devotional is a humbling reminder of his transformative grace. It's perfect for every teenager's walk with Christ!"

Dr. Joe White, President, Kanakuk Ministries

"A highly recommended, valuable contribution to teenagers and the church. This devotional cuts against the grain of standard teen devotionals, which historically point kids to their own inner strength. This devotional points kids to Jesus and his finished work. It also offers practical instruction on spiritual disciplines in a clear, helpful, non-legalistic way."

Cameron Cole, Chairman of Rooted: Advancing Grace-Driven Ministry; director of youth ministries, Cathedral Church of the Advent, Birmingham, AL; coeditor, *Gospel-Centered Youth Ministry*

"The Bible, from Genesis to Revelation, is not a story about us but about Jesus. The way teenagers begin to understand themselves is to get caught up in a story bigger than their own. Kristen Hatton has captured a unique, clever, and devotional way to grab the hearts and minds of young men and women. For those of us who work with college students, our plea would be: please give this book to teenagers a few years before they hit the college campus. They will come better prepared to face campus life and pressure. They will be men and women who understand that their life and story is defined by his story."

Rod Mays, Former National Coordinator, Reformed University Fellowship

"*Get Your Story Straight* is a powerful way to introduce teenagers to God's Word. The difference between *Get Your Story Straight* and other devotions for teens is that it goes through the Bible from beginning to end and reveals truths in stories from the Old and New Testament in a new, exciting way that they can relate to. Readers of this devotional are introduced to biblical principles like justification and sanctification—life-changing truths of what Jesus offers through the sacrifice he made for us on the cross. I would recommend *Get Your Story Straight* to any teen."

Lauren Nelson, Miss America 2007; author

"Raising kids in today's society to honor God and to invest in his kingdom can be a challenge. *Get Your Story Straight* is a great tool to encourage young people to find their true identity in Jesus and pursue him passionately."

Lance Berkman, Former Major League Baseball player

"The story about Jesus and the gospel isn't just a point in history. It is the history of thousands of years of love and hate, joy and sadness, victory and loss, all of which gets us ready for the greatest climax of the greatest story ever told. It's also the story that becomes our story when we see ourselves written into the purposes of God in the pages of Scripture. Kristen Hatton has done us a big favor by making the storyline clear and the applications personal and relevant. I wish my wife and I had this book when our children were teenagers."

Dr. Joseph (Skip) Ryan

"Finally, a devotional that connects youth to the substance and story of the Bible! Kristen Hatton has given teenagers a gift in *Get Your Story Straight*—with key Scripture passages to memorize, thoughtful questions to fuel reflection, and gospel application. Take up and read!"

Brian H. Cosby, Author, *Giving Up Gimmicks: Reclaiming Youth Ministry from an Entertainment Culture*

"Kristen Hatton in her book has struck just the right balance for a teen who is a new believer or is a searcher to learn and understand God's Word and the gospel. The readings are Bible-based and present the story in daily doses that build on content and repetition so that a solid Christian world and life view is firmly established."

Brad Bradley, Founder, Southwest Church Planting Network

"If you view the Christian life as being about your performance, then what do you do if you are not performing well? Regrettably, many Christians never follow an inductive Bible study or develop the daily exercise of meditating on the greatest story ever told. This incredible step-by-step guide to learning and living the gospel of Jesus Christ will help not only teens to approach the Bible but adults as well. Led by this devotional, become captivated by the narrative and the characters in God's story as you rest in the words of Jesus when he says, 'It is finished.'"

Mark Davis, Senior Pastor, Park Cities Presbyterian Church, Dallas, TX

"What an outstanding job Kristen Hatton has done crafting a devotional that makes the Scriptures wonderfully accessible to modern teens. It invites them to study the ancient biblical narrative so they discover the life-transforming reality of the One who is at the center of that narrative. And in so doing, it encourages them to make sense of their 'story' in light of THE story."

Leo R. Schuster III, Lead Pastor, City Church, Houston, TX

"Teaching the next generation to understand how their story intersects with the grand story of the Bible is mission critical for the church. Kristen Hatton offers an engaging, relevant, and Word-saturated tool for this high and holy calling."

Karen Hodge, PCA Women's Ministry Coordinator

"As teenagers, we make the most important decisions in our lives. We decide who we will be, where we are going, and who we are taking with us, all before we reach adulthood. That thought scares me. If we want teens to make right choices, they need to know who they are. They need to know how they fit into God's story. Kristen Hatton's book aims to teach them that very thing. As we learn who God is and where he plans to take this world, we begin to see the way to follow him. I am confident this book will help teenagers of all ages and I commend it to you warmly."

Ricky Jones, Pastor, RiverOaks Presbyterian Church, Tulsa, OK

"God's call on my life came when I was a teenager, so teens have always been at the heart of my ministry. Following seminary, the first opportunity the Lord gave me to serve was as a youth pastor. I learned firsthand the importance of a walk with the Lord in the formative years of adolescence. Kristen Hatton speaks directly to the minds and hearts of teenagers with truth and grace. These young men and women, especially in today's culture, need a daily reminder of God's authority, his sovereignty, and his grace in a relatable way. This little book carries that big message!"

Ed Young, Senior Pastor, Second Baptist Church, Houston, TX

"Kristen has taken Scripture and made it accessible for teenagers in a culture that tells them to tune out and disengage. She challenges teens to take the next step beyond just reading the Bible. This study was written with them in mind; it allows them to engage Scripture in different ways throughout the week, helping Scripture come alive. Teenagers at any point in their relationship with Christ can use this book to help them grow in their faith and understanding of who Jesus is."

Sydney Miller, Young Life Director, Edmond, OK

Get Your Story Straight

A Teen's Guide to Learning and Living the Gospel

Kristen Hatton

New
Growth
Press
www.newgrowthpress.com

New Growth Press, Greensboro, NC 27404
www.newgrowthpress.com
Copyright © 2015 by Kristen Hatton

Unless otherwise indicated, Scripture quotations are taken from
The Holy Bible, English Standard Version.® Copyright © 2000;
2001 by Crossway Bibles, a division of Good News Publishers.
Used by permission. All rights reserved.

Cover Design: Faceout Books, faceoutstudio.com
Typesetting and eBook: Lisa Parnell, lparnell.com

ISBN: 978-1-942572-06-0 (Print)
ISBN: 978-1-942572-07-7 (eBook)

Printed in the United States of America

25 24 23 22 21 20 19 18   3 4 5 6 7

Dear Rebecca,

As my only daughter and first teenager,
you were the motivation behind this book.
I love you so much and am blessed beyond measure
the Lord gave you to "Padre" and me.

Contents

Foreword

As a father of two teenagers and a preteen, as a coach and teacher at a Christian school, as a campus minister at a Christian university, and now a church planter, one thing has become very clear to me: a large percentage of the teenagers who profess to be Christians know little about the faith they profess to believe. From my experience, students may know some Bible verses, but they don't know the story of the Bible. They don't know how they fit into the story of a redeeming King and his kingdom, so many are ill-equipped to deal with real life in this broken, sinful, fallen world.

Too many Christians view the Bible either as an instruction manual on how to get to heaven, or maybe a bunch of moral stories showing us how to live a moral, godly life, or even as an encyclopedic record of a lot of information on a host of unrelated topics. But most are not sure how, or if, it all fits together. When we approach the Bible in these ways, we miss seeing the glory of who Jesus is and all that he has done for us. When we miss seeing the worth of who Jesus is and the work he has done to save us, Christianity becomes a religion of rules and regulations focusing on our performance and ability to live a "good" Christian life.

Teenagers, if the Christian life is all about you and your performance, where do you turn when you aren't performing well? Do you know how to deal honestly with your sin? Do you know how to find comfort and hope in the gospel? Do you know how to rest in Jesus's words, "*It is finished,*" or are you running on the performance treadmill believing you must put in more effort to finish?

My wife has written this devotional book for you. It will help you find your life as you get lost in the story of Jesus. My prayer for you as you read this devotional is that the love God has for you in Christ would become real to you—that who Jesus is and all he has done for you would transform your life so much that you will begin to display Jesus in the way you live with others.

— Pete Hatton

Introduction

Did you know that we all live out of some story? Whether it's a story about our successes, our failures, who our friends are, or what we have accomplished (or not accomplished), we all have a story that helps us make sense of our lives and our world. Perhaps you have heard about the story of Jesus, but his story seems pretty disconnected from your real life—the life where friends, appearance, academics, athletics, activities, accomplishments, dating, parties, etc., take up your time and attention. At the same time, you might be wishing for a different life and a different approach to your problems. You might have already noticed that no matter how hard you try to make yourself feel happy, fulfilled, and worthwhile, you still struggle with dissatisfaction and emptiness. The solution is not to go have more fun, get out of your house, or change your situation; instead it's to get your story straight. Living out of the true story—the story of the gospel of Jesus Christ—will change your life from the inside out.

Do you know that story? Many people have a hard time answering this basic question of Christianity: What is the gospel? Perhaps that's true for you as well. This book was written to help you understand the gospel, but even more than that to introduce the hero of the story—Jesus. Getting to know Jesus will change your life right now and give you life forever.

As you go through this book, you will notice that we start the story from the beginning. That's always the best way to get your story straight! The beginning of the story will explain why our problems are much deeper than our outward behavior and why following Jesus takes more than going to church or trying to do the "right thing." Instead, we will see that our problems start with what is going on inside of us—what we want, desire, and live for. As you understand yourself better, you will also find out how much you need Jesus every day.

The devotionals in this book will lead you through the whole Bible so that you can understand the complete unfolding story of the gospel. Through this grid you will learn who Jesus is and why we need him, and that knowledge will shape your understanding of freedom and grace, growth in love for God and people, and how the gospel changes everything. While this yearlong study was designed for individual devotional times, a small group or parent/teen dialogue alongside it could be helpful. Either way, it would be great for you to have someone to talk with about what you are learning.

For each of the fifty-two weeks, there are devotions for five days that concentrate on the same passage of Scripture. The intent is that through repetitive reading and in-depth focused time, the unfolding truths of the lesson will go deeper into your life than if that section of the Bible was simply read once. So you will notice that you are encouraged to read the same Scripture passage several times throughout the week. Day One of each week is focused on examining the text through observations that will aid you in discovering what is being revealed in the passage. This includes exercises like identifying repetitive key words, clauses, or action verbs, as well as asking probing questions to help make inferences beyond what is simply stated in the text. An example passage with inductive study questions and answers can be found in the next section titled "Day One Aid: How to Study the Bible."

By approaching Scripture this same way week after week, an added benefit is that you will be able to develop a Bible study method to carry you through life. You will spend the second day reading the written devotional material and the third and fourth days answering questions that unpack the passage and devotional reading. Day Five concludes in prayer after you spend time journaling. In addition, each of the three parts of the book begins with a memory verse for you to learn over the course of that section.

The lessons build on each other—so don't skip around! You have to follow the story from the beginning to end. This devotional is meant to last a whole year, but you may go through it faster or slower. The important thing is to keep going.

As you get started, my prayer for you is that the story of God's glory and amazing grace will take root, transforming your heart and changing your desires, thoughts, and behaviors. Along the way, you will find that your everyday life has become rich in the things that matter most—faith, hope, and love.

Day One Aid
How to Study the Bible

As discussed in the Introduction, Day One of each week uses an inductive study method to approach each passage. This method of Bible study is called *inductive* because you will make observations and notice details to help you gain greater insight into what is being communicated in the Scripture. This is a great way to look at any passage, and I hope you find it helpful beyond this book.

I have included a Day One sample here as a guide for working through the first day's instructions. The passage below is not otherwise included in the book, but the exercises here will show you the types of observations and answers you will be looking for. Don't get frustrated or hung up on getting it all "right." No one is grading your work. You will benefit more from each devotional if you spend the time slowly reading the Scripture, working through the Day One exercises, and going back to reread the passage as instructed on Days Three and Four.

To practice, read the Mark passage below and try to answer the listed questions before looking at the included responses to each instruction. Also note that not all of these instructions will be given for any one week, and there may be other questions more fitting for certain passages.

Straight from the Word
Read the Scripture and follow the instructions below.

:: Mark 4:35–41

35 On that day, when evening had come, he [Jesus] said to them [his disciples], "Let us go across to the other side." 36 And leaving the crowd, they took him with them in the boat, just as he was. And other boats were with him. 37 And a great windstorm arose, and the waves were

breaking into the boat, so that the boat was already filling. [38] But he was in the stern, asleep on the cushion. And they woke him and said to him, "Teacher, do you not care that we are perishing?" [39] And he awoke and rebuked the wind and said to the sea, "Peace! Be still!" And the wind ceased, and there was a great calm. [40] He said to them, "Why are you so afraid? Have you still no faith?" [41] And they were filled with great fear and said to one another, "Who then is this, that even the wind and the sea obey him?"

:: Make five or more observations from the passages.
  ~ The storm is so strong the boat is filling with water.
  ~ Seems surprising Jesus could sleep in that heavy of a storm.
  ~ Jesus is at the stern, which means he is the one in control of the boat.
  ~ The disciples think they are going to die in the storm.
  ~ Like in creation, Jesus speaks and what he commands happens.
  ~ Jesus confronts them with their fears and doubts when he is in control!

:: What is the conflict?
  ~ The storm has stirred up fear in the disciples' hearts, and Jesus isn't doing anything about it.

:: What is the climax?
  ~ Jesus tells the wind and sea to be still and they are.

:: Summarize the main idea.
  ~ We fear the things we can't control, yet Jesus shows us what being calm amid the storm looks like.

:: Write down any thoughts or questions.
  ~ The disciples' question to Jesus—doesn't he care they are perishing?—seems to show a lack of trust; they doubt he really cares about them.
  ~ The storm is used to reveal the fear the disciples felt.
  ~ Based on verse 41, do the disciples really not believe he is the Messiah?

~ Are we like the disciples in thinking if God really cared he wouldn't allow storms to happen?

Making your own observations and inquiries at the beginning of each week builds a foundation for further study that will help shape and lead you to all the Lord wants you to see in his Word. As you commit yourself to discovering more of who he is and seeing his great love for you, may the "word of Christ dwell in you richly" (Colossians 3:16).

PART I

Getting the Story Straight

Scripture Memory:

"You search the Scriptures because you think that in them you have eternal life; and it is they that bear witness about me."
(John 5:39)

Week 1

Whose Story Is It?

DAY ONE
Straight from the Word

Read the Scripture and follow the instructions below.

:: Genesis 1:1–2

[1] In the beginning, God created the heavens and the earth. [2] The earth was without form and void, and darkness was over the face of the deep. And the Spirit of God was hovering over the face of the waters.

:: John 1:1–5

[1] In the beginning was the Word [Jesus is the Word], and the Word was with God, and the Word was God. [2] He was in the beginning with God. [3] All things were made through him, and without him was not any thing made that was made. [4] In him was life, and the life was the light of men. [5] The light shines in the darkness, and the darkness has not overcome it.

:: Hebrews 1:1–3

[1] Long ago, at many times and in many ways, God spoke to our fathers by the prophets, [2] but in these last days he has spoken to us by his Son, whom he appointed the heir of all things, through whom also he created the world. [3] He is the radiance of the glory of God and the

exact imprint of his nature, and he upholds the universe by the word of his power.

:: Make five observations from the passages.

:: What connection do you see between these three passages?

:: Summarize the main idea of the passages.

:: Write down any thoughts or questions.

DAY TWO
The Word Applied

How often do you become so engrossed in a TV series that you watch multiple seasons in a matter of days or weeks? Our family had a show like that. Every possible night we were all home, without sports or other activities, we settled into our favorite seats in front of the television to jump back into the lives of these characters that had become our friends. Even in conversations I found myself relating friends' real-life situations back to the events going on in my pseudo-friends' lives!

Some shows are like that and you just can't wait for the next episode. Or it may be the book you can't put down. Why is it we become so captivated by stories?

It could be you identify with one of the characters, or perhaps it's the intensity of the drama or the emotions you feel. But I believe we become enamored because in our human DNA we were made to find our life by getting caught up in the story of another. Not just any story, but God created us to get lost in his story.

The Bible is his story. It's a storybook, not a textbook. From Genesis to Revelation it's a story about creation's King and his grand design for the world he created. The stage is set in Genesis 1:1 by immediately proclaiming who the main character of the story is: "In the beginning GOD . . ." Notice it does not say, "In the beginning man." And again in John: "In the beginning was the Word . . ." The Word who is Creator of all things, heir of all things, upholder of all things, and the One through whom God speaks to us is Jesus!

We get the story wrong when we put ourselves center stage. When we come to the Bible focused on us and not him, God becomes our "stage hand" to give us what we want, when we want it, in the way we want it. When that happens we miss rightly understanding who he is, and we never get caught up in his story.

This devotional book is designed to challenge you to look for this King and what the Bible tells you about him, instead of reading Scripture primarily for how it applies directly to you. This eternal King who breathed life into creation is the same King who gives life and meaning to all things. This means no matter your age, where you live, who your family is, or what your past includes, God wants you to experience the freedom of being secure in his great love—the love revealed for you in the story of his Son. Allow him to occupy his rightful place on the throne of your heart.

DAY THREE _____

Straight to My Heart

Before answering the questions, reread the Scripture, being mindful of insights from the first two days.

:: What do you see right from the start about who God is?

:: What does it mean to get caught up in the story of the Bible?

:: Why do you think when we study the Bible we tend to miss Jesus in the story?

DAY FOUR   _____

Word and Deed

Reread the Scripture one more time and then take your time answering the questions below.

:: What is the danger in not seeing the entire story of the Bible as Jesus's unfolding story?

:: If God occupied his rightful place as the most important person in your life and the center of your world, how would that change today? Next week? This year?

:: What opportunities do you have right now to share God's story (both in what you say and do) with others?

DAY FIVE _____

Journaling and Prayer

:: What struck you from this week's lesson? How have you seen the Bible differently?

Spend time writing your thoughts.

Prayer

Lord, help me get caught up in your story. Help me to see that it's all about you not me, so that by seeing you I might come to understand and know you better.

Week 2

Creation's King

DAY ONE

Straight from the Word

Read the Scripture and follow the instructions below.

:: Genesis 1:3–31

³ And God said, "Let there be light," and there was light. ⁴ And God saw that the light was good. And God separated the light from the darkness. . . . ⁶ And God said, "Let there be an expanse in the midst of the waters, and let it separate the waters from the waters. . . ." ⁹ And God said, "Let the waters under the heavens be gathered together into one place, and let the dry land appear." And it was so. . . . ¹¹ And God said, "Let the earth sprout vegetation, plants yielding seed, and fruit trees . . . each according to its kind, on the earth. . . ."

¹⁴ And God said, "Let there be lights in the expanse of the heavens to separate the day from the night. And let them be for signs and for seasons, and for days and years. . . ." ¹⁶ And God made the two great lights—the greater light to rule the day and the lesser light to rule the night—and the stars. . . . ²⁰ And God said, "Let the waters swarm with swarms of living creatures, and let birds fly above the earth across the expanse of the heavens. . . ." ²⁴ And God said, "Let the earth bring forth living creatures . . . livestock and creeping things and beasts of the earth. . . ." And it was so. . . .

²⁶ Then God said, "Let us make man in our image, after our likeness. And let them have dominion over the fish of the sea and over the birds of the heavens and over the livestock and over all the earth and over every creeping thing that creeps on the earth." ²⁷ So God created man in his own image, in the image of God he created him; male and female he created them. ²⁸ And God blessed them. And God said to them, "Be fruitful and multiply and fill the earth and subdue it, and have dominion over the fish of the sea and over the birds of the heavens and over every living thing that moves on the earth." ²⁹ And God said, "Behold, I have given you every plant yielding seed that is on the face of all the earth, and every tree with seed in its fruit. You shall have them for food. . . . ³¹ And God saw everything that he had made, and behold, it was very good. And there was evening and there was morning, the sixth day.

:: Circle the main action verbs.

:: Who is doing the action?

:: Summarize the main idea.

:: Write down any thoughts or questions.

DAY TWO

The Word Applied

In the beginning, God is revealed as master architect and builder with all of creation his royal construction site.[1] As he gives shape, form, and light to the empty darkness, the foundation is set for a home to his people. Then in giving order and hierarchy to the realms of the sky, sea, and land, his pattern of design is imprinted on man who is called to rule as he does.

Stop and think about this: the King of the universe gave us (humans) authority over all he had made—crowned with value and worth, purpose and privilege to rule over all creation. How special must we be in his sight to be viewed as princes and princesses by the supreme King!

God made people to be over all things, yet still under his ultimate authority and sovereign purposes. This is hard for us to grasp because we desire independence and control. We think freedom comes in not being under the authority of anyone else. For example, you may want out from under your parents' rules, for teachers' assignments not to dictate your days, or for a boss not to demand you work an evening that interferes with social plans.

This is not how it was in the garden. Adam and Eve relished their special bond with God, completely satisfied by being in submission to him. They understood that dependence on God was what it meant to be human. But often we think just the opposite. We feel as if dependence restrains us, so we try to live as if we don't need God or others.

If only we could grasp that when God declared "It is good," it was supremely good. There was nothing lacking and nothing Adam and Eve wished was different. They felt perfectly loved, cared for, and free. Free to perform and live as God designed, with no wants or unmet desires. Imagine living that way—where everything is good and operates as it was designed and where men and women perfectly reflect God's image as holy and perfect.

DAY THREE

Straight to My Heart

Before answering the questions, reread the Scripture, being mindful of insights from the first two days.

:: List all you learn about who God is through the creation.

:: Why was God's authority over Adam and Eve a good thing?

:: What does it look like to live dependent on God?

DAY FOUR
Back to the Word

Reread the Scripture one more time and then take your time answering the questions below.

:: What areas in your life do you seek to control, trying to be your own authority and not living under God's rule?

:: List some reasons that you would like to control your own life instead of being under God's control.

:: How might today be different if by God's grace you accepted his authority over your time, your relationships, your money?

DAY FIVE

Journaling and Prayer

:: Take yourself back to the garden when all was good. How would your relationships with your family and friends look different than they do now?

Spend time writing your thoughts.

Prayer

Lord, you are Creator King of the world and love me as your child. Help me to see your authority over all things as your love for me.

Week 3

In His Image

DAY ONE
Straight from the Word

Read the Scripture and then follow the instructions below.

:: Genesis 2:18–25

[18] Then the LORD God said, "It is not good that the man should be alone; I will make him a helper fit for him." [19] Now out of the ground the LORD God had formed every beast of the field and every bird of the heavens and brought them to the man to see what he would call them. And whatever the man called every living creature, that was its name. [20] The man gave names to all livestock and to the birds of the heavens and to every beast of the field. But for Adam there was not found a helper fit for him. [21] So the LORD God caused a deep sleep to fall upon the man, and while he slept took one of his ribs and closed up its place with flesh. [22] And the rib that the LORD God had taken from the man he made into a woman and brought her to the man. [23] Then the man said, "This at last is bone of my bones and flesh of my flesh; she shall be called Woman, because she was taken out of Man." [24] Therefore a man shall leave his father and his mother and hold fast to his wife, and they shall become one flesh. [25] And the man and his wife were both naked and were not ashamed.

:: What similar actions to God does Adam perform?

:: What is the significance in this similarity?

:: What is the main idea of the passage?

:: Write down any thoughts or questions.

DAY TWO

The Word Applied

Why do you think God thought it was not good for man to be alone?

Do you think he felt sorry for Adam not having a partner like the animals did? Must we be married in order to not be lonely? Was Adam's relationship with God not enough?

As we saw last week in God creating man in his image, we were given all the characteristics and qualities to perfectly emulate who God is. But who was Adam to emulate God to without another person? It is for this reason God said it was not good for man to be alone. Man needed someone to reflect God back to.

Being made in the image of God means we were made for relationship because God is relationship. In the Trinity there is a loving community between the Father, Son, and Holy Spirit. C. S. Lewis in his book *Mere Christianity* calls it a dance: "In Christianity God is not a static thing . . . but a dynamic, pulsating activity, a life, almost a kind of a drama. Almost, if you will not think me irreverent, a kind of dance."[2]

Theologian Cornelius Plantinga expounded on this concept by showing how all three members of the Trinity seek to exalt, glorify, and serve the others. Just envision the Father orbiting around the Son seeking to glorify and honor him, while the Son radiates the Father's love by giving up his life in order to bring all of us to the Father. And the Spirit revolves around both the Father and the Son, illuminating their truth to us. Each person of the Trinity finds the greatest joy in exalting and submitting to another. It's a picture of perfect relational harmony.[3]

Therefore, God said, "It is not good that man should be alone" because it was not good for man not to have another image bearer to whom he could shine forth who God is. So with the creation of Eve, God's image became more visibly seen as man could join in the "dance" of revolving their lives around the good of another. This runs counter-cultural to the self-focused and self-first mind-set of the world. We take pride in our individualistic ways and often isolate ourselves from others. In doing so we miss seeing God's image displayed through us and to us.

Consider though what this higher calling for relationships might look like in your life. Instead of wanting to be recognized as the best on your team, you elevate someone else. Instead of retreating to your bedroom and closing the door, you offer to help your parent with some chores. Instead of being consumed with your phone, you engage in conversation with whomever you are with. Instead of hoarding the last of the ice cream, you offer it to your younger sibling. Instead of posting your party pictures on social media, you refrain so as not to hurt a friend who wasn't included. By exalting another over your own desires and seeking their good, you are dancing in the image of God!

DAY THREE

Straight to My Heart

Before answering the questions, reread the Scripture, being mindful of insights from the first two days.

:: What does it mean to be made in God's image?

:: What was God's intention for man not being alone?

:: When do you notice it to be challenging to "dance" around others, preferring instead life revolve around you?

DAY FOUR _____
Back to the Word

Reread the Scripture one more time and then take your time answering the questions below.

:: How would your relationships be affected by a genuine desire to better reflect God to others?

:: Consider what is going on in the lives of those around you this week. How can you reach out to love or serve a family member or friend today?

Take some time to prayerfully ask God for the opportunity to reach out!

DAY FIVE

Journaling and Prayer

:: Think about when you have reflected God's image to someone else and write about the situation/experience. How did it make you feel? How did the other person respond?

Prayer

Lord, help me glorify you in my relationships by the way I love and serve others above myself. And cause me to see when I have stopped "dancing" around others, desiring them to "dance" around me instead.

Week 4

World Turned on Its Head

DAY ONE

Straight from the Word

Read the Scripture and then follow the instructions below.

:: Genesis 2:16–17

¹⁶ And the Lord God commanded the man, saying, "You may surely eat of every tree of the garden, ¹⁷ but of the tree of the knowledge of good and evil you shall not eat, for in the day that you eat of it you shall surely die."

:: Genesis 3:1–7

¹ Now the serpent was more crafty than any other beast of the field that the Lord God had made. He said to the woman, "Did God actually say, 'You shall not eat of any tree in the garden'?" ² And the woman said to the serpent, "We may eat of the fruit of the trees in the garden, ³ but God said, 'You shall not eat of the fruit of the tree that is in the midst of the garden, neither shall you touch it, lest you die.'" ⁴ But the serpent said to the woman, "You will not surely die. ⁵ For God knows that when you eat of it your eyes will be opened, and you will be like God, knowing good and evil." ⁶ So when the woman saw that the tree was good for food, and that it was a delight to the eyes,

and that the tree was to be desired to make one wise, she took of its fruit and ate, and she also gave some to her husband who was with her, and he ate. [7] Then the eyes of both were opened, and they knew that they were naked. And they sewed fig leaves together and made themselves loincloths.

:: Circle the repetitive words in the passage (e.g., eyes).

:: Make a list of observations based off the repetitive words you found.

:: In verse 6, what reasons are given for Eve deciding to eat the fruit?

:: Write down any thoughts or questions.

DAY TWO
The Word Applied

A text message circulates around school with the details of a party being thrown by a classmate whose parents are out of town. You know there will be drinking and probably drugs there too, and there is no way your parents would ever let you go. But all your friends will be there and you don't want to miss out. They finally convince you that your parents won't find out, so you rationalize that because you aren't going to drink it will be okay to go this one time.

Sounds a little like the rationalization of Adam and Eve. That one tree, that one little piece of fruit off it—surely one bite wouldn't matter. Kind of like going to the party—just this once it won't be a big deal. It's easy to justify that hiding it from your parents is okay.

Eve may have been thinking along those same lines. But on top of that, she thought God was holding out on her. Of course, God did not want her to eat of that tree if it meant she would be like him! But she was missing a huge truth: She was already like God! She was created perfect, holy, righteous, and without sin. She enjoyed complete satisfaction in her relationship with Adam, and together they ruled God's kingdom perfectly, imaging him.

That all changed when she took the fruit. No longer were Adam and Eve like God. No longer was it "on earth as it is in heaven." Eve's action affected all of creation permanently. With that bite, God's image in man was broken. As we talked about last week, now instead of being others-centered, we became self-centered. Instead of serving others for their good, we demand to be served. Instead of laying down our lives for another, we are more concerned with doing what's best for ourselves. Instead of seeing dependency on God as life giving, we fight to be self-sufficient. Instead of seeking God's glory, we want to be exalted.

When sin entered the world, it was more than breaking God's rules (remember those haven't even been given yet in Genesis 3!). Sin at its core is living independently from God. Sin is living for self. When the Bible says "their eyes were opened," this is what our eyes were opened to—a sin nature that turned the world on its head and led Adam and Eve to see their shame that needed covering.

DAY THREE
Straight to My Heart

Before answering the questions, reread the Scripture, being mindful of insights from the first two days.

:: Do you ever feel like God is holding out from giving you his best? If so, how?

:: In what ways and why do you sometimes rationalize your behavior or activities?

:: What does it mean that God's image in man was broken when Adam and Eve took the fruit?

DAY FOUR

Back to the Word

Reread the Scripture one more time and then take your time answering the questions below.

:: How has this lesson expanded your view of what sin is?

:: Why is being others-centered so hard?

:: How is being more mindful of others than yourself possible?

DAY FIVE

Journaling and Prayer

:: If sin is living independently from God, spend some time today writing a prayer of confession for the ways you try to live your life apart from him.

Prayer

Lord, help me to see the depth of my sin in the ways I seek to live independently of you.

Week 5

Hide and Seek

DAY ONE

Straight from the Word

Read the Scripture and then follow the instructions below.

:: Genesis 3:8–21

⁸ And they heard the sound of the LORD God walking in the garden in the cool of the day, and the man and his wife hid themselves from the presence of the LORD God among the trees of the garden. ⁹ But the LORD God called to the man and said to him, "Where are you?" ¹⁰ And he said, "I heard the sound of you in the garden, and I was afraid, because I was naked, and I hid myself." ¹¹ He said, "Who told you that you were naked? Have you eaten of the tree of which I commanded you not to eat?" ¹² The man said, "The woman whom you gave to be with me, she gave me fruit of the tree, and I ate." ¹³ Then the LORD God said to the woman, "What is this that you have done?" The woman said, "The serpent deceived me, and I ate."

¹⁴ The LORD God said to the serpent, "Because you have done this, cursed are you above all livestock and above all beasts of the field; on your belly you shall go, and dust you shall eat all the days of your life. ¹⁵ I will put enmity between you and the woman, and between your offspring and her offspring; he shall bruise your head, and you shall bruise his heel."

¹⁶ To the woman he said, "I will surely multiply your pain in child-bearing; in pain you shall bring forth children. Your desire shall be for your husband, and he shall rule over you."

¹⁷ And to Adam he said, "Because you have listened to the voice of your wife and have eaten of the tree of which I commanded you, 'You shall not eat of it,' cursed is the ground because of you; in pain you shall eat of it all the days of your life; ¹⁸ thorns and thistles it shall bring forth for you; and you shall eat the plants of the field. ¹⁹ By the sweat of your face you shall eat bread, till you return to the ground, for out of it you were taken; for you are dust, and to dust you shall return." ²⁰ The man called his wife's name Eve, because she was the mother of all living. ²¹ And the LORD God made for Adam and for his wife garments of skins and clothed them.

:: Underline each of the accusations (not questions) made in the passage.

:: What do you notice about these accusations?

:: Summarize the main idea.

:: Write down any thoughts or questions.

DAY TWO
The Word Applied

Kara bought a top her parents would deem inappropriate. Everyone else is wearing this style though, and it really doesn't seem bad. But in order to leave the house, she puts a hoodie over it and then sheds the jacket at school.

Jonathan has been anxious to check out the website his friends have been talking about, so he waits until his family leaves home to go online. After spending an hour surfing from one link to another, he wipes clean the evidence from the computer's history.

In both situations what was done is what Adam and Eve did too. They hid. They knew what they had done was wrong and they were afraid. Previously they were naked and unashamed, but now they feel exposed in their nakedness. This is because their eyes had been opened to sin, and in their shame they knew they need covering.

Sewing fig leaves together for clothing sounds like a lot of trouble. And to make the clothing quickly enough to cover themselves before God came into the garden took fast thinking. We do that type of thing in our sin too. We go to a lot of trouble sometimes to cover up our shame and to keep from being exposed.

What is amazing is how God dealt with them in their sin. In God's original command not to eat from the particular tree he said, "The day you eat of it you shall surely die." While life-altering consequences changed the course of the world, Adam and Eve didn't die—at least not an immediate physical death like they might have assumed.

God not only spared their lives, but he clothed them properly with an animal's skin. Getting that skin required an animal to die. Do you see what this means?

God in his infinite love and grace refused to make Adam and Eve pay with their lives, but he sacrificed an animal in their place, using its skin to cover them in their shame. What a beautiful picture of what Christ did for us as the ultimate sacrifice! He received our payment by dying in our place and clothed us with his righteousness even though we did nothing to deserve it.

Jesus came not to condemn us in our sin but to seek and save what was lost in the garden. This means you do not have to hide from God and try to cover your own shame by good works or lies. You can freely confess, and God will embrace you. Amazing grace, how sweet the sound!

DAY THREE

Straight to My Heart

Before answering the questions, reread the Scripture, being mindful of insights from the first two days.

:: Why do you still try to cover up and hide in your sin?

:: How do you see God's grace to you even when there are still consequences for confessed sin?

:: What does Genesis 3 show you about who God is?

DAY FOUR
Back to the Word

Reread the Scripture one more time and then take your time answering the questions below.

:: How does God covering Adam and Eve with the skin of a sacrificed animal depict what Christ does for us?

:: How should remembering your covering by Christ's righteousness help you live more freely?

:: How should remembering others are also covered by Christ's righteousness help you extend grace to them in their sin?

DAY FIVE

Journaling and Prayer

:: Reflect on how you would relate differently to God if you did not fear him or feel like you have to hide your sin from him.

Spend time writing your thoughts.

Prayer

Lord, thank you for dying for my sins and covering me in your righteousness when I was the one who deserved death.

Week 6

Quest for Rest

DAY ONE

Straight from the Word

Read the Scripture and then follow the instructions below.

:: Genesis 2:1–3

[1] Thus the heavens and the earth were finished, and all the host of them.
[2] And on the seventh day God finished his work that he had done, and
he rested on the seventh day from all his work that he had done. [3] So
God blessed the seventh day and made it holy, because on it God rested
from all his work that he had done in creation.

:: Matthew 11:25–30

[25] At that time Jesus declared, "I thank you, Father, Lord of heaven
and earth, that you have hidden these things from the wise and understanding and revealed them to little children; [26] yes, Father, for such
was your gracious will. [27] All things have been handed over to me
by my Father, and no one knows the Son except the Father, and no
one knows the Father except the Son and anyone to whom the Son
chooses to reveal him. [28] Come to me, all who labor and are heavy
laden, and I will give you rest. [29] Take my yoke upon you, and learn
from me, for I am gentle and lowly in heart, and you will find rest for
your souls. [30] For my yoke is easy, and my burden is light."

:: Circle the key word appearing in both passages.

:: Underline the phrases indicating why God rested.

:: What does Jesus offer in his command to come to him?

:: Why does he offer us this?

DAY TWO

The Word Applied

During finals week, what is the only thing you want (besides good grades)? To be done—finished studying—and to have a break, right? Whether it's fall break, the Christmas holidays, spring break, or summer, it's always nice to have time off from the normal routine. Even if it's just the change of pace of a down weekend. Similarly, a college student may just want to graduate and be done with school permanently. A working adult may long to retire. Whatever the context, we strive for rest.

This connects back to the pattern set before us by God. For six days God worked creating the world, and on the seventh day, the Sabbath, he rested. This is not about God being tired. This is God sitting on his throne enjoying all that he had done, delighting in his creation—100 percent completely satisfied.

Until Adam and Eve sinned.

In that moment mankind lost God's favor, and with it came a never-satisfied thirst for more and a never-ending quest for rest. Rest in this context is being at peace with God, having his favor. This "rest" is the deepest longing of the human heart. Though we may not realize it to be the root of our struggles, it is a longing never satisfied because of sin.

It's like eating breakfast to satisfy your morning hunger. You are full for a few hours, but it doesn't last. Come lunchtime your stomach is rumbling and ready for more food. That is the insatiable appetite of longing for rest. Nothing totally and completely satisfies.

Nevertheless, we continue in our restlessness because we forget we already have his favor. Instead of turning to him in our sin, we try to outweigh it by doing "good" as a means of making it up to God. Instead of trusting that his perfect obedience was a sufficient covering, we fall back to basing how well we are doing as a Christian on our own ability to please God. Instead of going to him with all our worries, doubts, and struggles, we try to manage and control it ourselves. Adam's failure sent mankind into this tailspin frenzy of looking to our own efforts to regain God's favor because we don't think we have it.

Are you tired of trying to get what you already have? Step off the running treadmill of believing you have to perform and rest in his performance for you. He delights in you. He is the Lord of the Sabbath and the only one who can give you true rest.

DAY THREE

Straight to My Heart

Before answering the questions, reread the Scripture being mindful of insights from the first two days.

:: Why are you insecure in God's love for you?

:: In what ways do you try to earn God's favor on your own?

:: How does Jesus fill our insatiable appetite for rest?

DAY FOUR   _____

Back to the Word

Reread the Scripture one more time and then take your time answering the questions below.

:: What does restlessness look like for you?

:: What would it look like if you rested in God's love knowing you could never lose it?

:: If you were securely resting in God's love, how would it affect your relationships?

DAY FIVE _____

Journaling and Prayer

:: Go back to Matthew 11:28–30 and spend some time thinking about what it really means to take his yoke upon you. (You may need to google the word "yoke.") Write about what this would mean for you when you are burdened or restless.

Prayer

Lord, help me to see where I misplace my longing for rest. In its place help me to understand that Jesus satisfied the work you required for us to receive once again your look of love and Sabbath rest.

Week 7

A Plan and a Promise

DAY ONE
Straight from the Word

Read the Scripture and then follow the instructions below.

:: Genesis 3:15

"I [God] will put enmity between you [Satan] and the woman, and between your offspring and her offspring; he shall bruise your head, and you shall bruise his heel."

:: Galatians 3:16–29

[16] Now the promises were made to Abraham and to his offspring. It does not say, "And to offsprings," referring to many, but referring to one, "And to your offspring," who is Christ. [17] This is what I mean: the law, which came 430 years afterward, does not annul a covenant previously ratified by God, so as to make the promise void. [18] For if the inheritance comes by the law, it no longer comes by promise; but God gave it to Abraham by a promise. [19] Why then the law? It was added because of transgressions, until the offspring should come to whom the promise had been made, and it was put in place through angels by an intermediary. [20] Now an intermediary implies more than one, but God is one. [21] Is the law then contrary to the promises of God? Certainly

not! For if a law had been given that could give life, then righteousness would indeed be by the law. 22 But the Scripture imprisoned everything under sin, so that the promise by faith in Jesus Christ might be given to those who believe. 23 Now before faith came, we were held captive under the law, imprisoned until the coming faith would be revealed. 24 So then, the law was our guardian until Christ came, in order that we might be justified by faith. 25 But now that faith has come, we are no longer under a guardian, 26 for in Christ Jesus you are all sons of God, through faith. 27 For as many of you as were baptized into Christ have put on Christ. 28 There is neither Jew nor Greek, there is neither slave nor free, there is no male and female, for you are all one in Christ Jesus. 29 And if you are Christ's, then you are Abraham's offspring, heirs according to promise.

:: Circle the word "offspring" every time it appears.

:: Between the two passages, which two offsprings are one and the same?

:: Underline all who are considered Abraham's offspring.

:: Write down any thoughts or questions.

DAY TWO
The Word Applied

Before a rose blooms, its petals are pressed tightly together concealing its full beauty. Only after it begins to open do you see its radiance. Genesis 3:15 is like a rosebud without the rest of the Bible to reveal what it truly means—the fullness of what is there will be missed! At this point we learn of the strife between two different offspring—that of the woman and that of Satan—but its significance has not yet been unfolded through Scripture's tracing of these two lines. However, it is essential to our understanding of the Bible that in this verse alone God proclaims his plan for the world.

To understand that plan we must see what God means when he says, "I will put enmity between you and the woman." According to the Merriam-Webster Dictionary the word *enmity* elicits "hostility," "mutual hatred," and "animosity."[4] This is a deep-seated hatred of the worst kind. And who is it between? The most evil and destructive enemy—Satan—and the woman Eve.

God is declaring permanent strife between the two. But it's not limited to just them. The next line tells us it will extend to each of their offspring or descendants. Here we have the beginning of two family lines that can be traced throughout the entire Old Testament and will continue until Christ's return. Throughout time, Satan is pitted against God's chosen people, the promised descendents of Abraham. There will be constant conflict, division, manipulation, and deceit—the animosity between the two.

These are the consequences of sin that we experience in a fallen world. You wonder why we all can't just get along; why there is so much drama and problems in your everyday world? This is why. It stems all the way back to Genesis when enmity was placed between the two "seeds"—the seed of the woman and the seed of Satan.

The last phrase in the verse reads, "He shall bruise your head and you shall bruise his heel." "You" is Satan, and "he" is Jesus. The visual image is Satan, the slithering snake, striking the heel of Jesus on the cross. Yet it is on the cross that Jesus crushes the serpent's head for all eternity!

Right here in the beginning of Genesis, God gives us a snapshot of what's to come: a promise to send a Redeemer to reverse the effects of the Fall that occurred when Adam and Eve took the fruit. Just look all around and you see the effects of the Fall—the sin, the suffering, the sickness, and the pain we all experience. The natural disasters that occur and even the fact that our clothes wear out and our cars break down. Nothing is as it should be, and as a result we don't have that ultimate peace or rest we long for. Though there are glimpses of it, one day Christ will fully restore everything to its perfect state.

DAY THREE _____

Straight to My Heart

Before answering the questions, reread the Scripture, being mindful of insights from the first two days.

:: In what ways are you experiencing the effects of the Fall?

:: Even though we suffer the consequences of sin, what is the hope given in this passage?

:: How do you see Jesus reversing the effects of the Fall even now?

DAY FOUR

Back to the Word

Reread the Scripture one more time and then take your time answering the questions below.

:: Why is your understanding of the unfolding of Genesis 3:15 crucial to how you interpret the Bible and view life?

:: What are the two different "seeds" or lines?

:: Open your Bible or Bible app on your phone to Luke 3:23–38 and read how Jesus's genealogy is traced back to the woman.

DAY FIVE

Journaling and Prayer

:: Reflect on what the Lord has been teaching you this week. How have you been challenged to view the Bible differently? Has your understanding changed or deepened?

Spend time writing your thoughts.

Prayer

Lord, thank you for promising us your Son, our Redeemer, who will make all things right again.

Week 8

The Best Witness Ever

DAY ONE
Straight from the Word

Read the Scripture and then follow the instructions below.

Note: In the John 5 passage, Jesus is having a heated conversation with the Jews over their problem with him healing on the Sabbath and declaring himself equal with God. He backs up his claim by three witnesses made known in the text, in which Jesus alludes to the 2 Peter passage.

:: John 5:31–44

31 "If I [Jesus] alone bear witness about myself, my testimony is not true. 32 There is another who bears witness about me, and I know that the testimony that he bears about me is true. 33 You sent to John [John the Baptist], and he has borne witness to the truth. 34 Not that the testimony that I receive is from man, but I say these things so that you may be saved. 35 He was a burning and shining lamp, and you were willing to rejoice for a while in his light. 36 But the testimony that I have is greater than that of John. For the works that the Father has given me to accomplish, the very works that I am doing, bear witness about me that the Father has sent me. 37 And the Father who sent me has himself borne witness about me. His voice you have never heard, his form you have never seen, 38 and you do not have his word abiding

in you, for you do not believe the one whom he has sent. [39] You search the Scriptures because you think that in them you have eternal life; and it is they that bear witness about me, [40] yet you refuse to come to me that you may have life. . . . [43] I have come in my Father's name, and you do not receive me. If another comes in his own name, you will receive him. [44] How can you believe, when you receive glory from one another and do not seek the glory that comes from the only God?"

:: 2 Peter 1:16–21

[16] For we [Peter and the apostles] did not follow cleverly devised myths when we made known to you [Christ followers] the power and coming of our Lord Jesus Christ, but we were eyewitnesses of his majesty. [17] For when he [Jesus] received honor and glory from God the Father, and the voice was borne to him by the Majestic Glory, "This is my beloved Son, with whom I am well pleased," [18] we ourselves heard this very voice borne from heaven, for we were with him on the holy mountain. [19] And we have the prophetic word more fully confirmed, to which you will do well to pay attention as to a lamp shining in a dark place . . . [20] knowing this first of all, that no prophecy of Scripture comes from someone's own interpretation. [21] For no prophecy was ever produced by the will of man, but men spoke from God as they were carried along by the Holy Spirit.

:: In the John passage, circle the three identified as bearing witness to Jesus.

:: List everything the passages say about Scripture.

:: Underline John 5:39 as it serves as the Scripture memory for Part I of this book.

:: Spend a few minutes working on memorizing it and then write it down below.

DAY TWO

The Word Applied

In America, as with many other nations, an accused person is presumed innocent until proven guilty. Therefore, the prosecutor must have enough evidence to convict, and the defendant has the right to witnesses testifying on his behalf. The witnesses are intended to lend credibility to the accused, perhaps as a character witness speaking to the type of person the defendant is. This is the type of scene we find ourselves in, but before the witnesses are introduced we need some background information.

Jesus has recently begun his public ministry of teaching and performing miracles. In this passage, he is talking to the Pharisees, who are the "righteous" Jewish law-keepers of the time. They know the "ins and outs" of the law and seek to enforce it on everyone. You can think of them as the "purity police," who are growing increasingly uneasy with the gathering of large crowds who believe Jesus is, in fact, the Son of God.

Jesus has just healed an ailing man, and the Pharisees complain that he shouldn't have done this "work" on the Sabbath day of rest. This serves as the catalyst to their anger boiling, but the real issue behind their outrage is Jesus's declaration that he is equal with God. According to the Pharisees, this blasphemous assertion put Jesus in need of a defense.

It's time for him to reveal his witnesses. He first names John the Baptist, who you can read more about in John 1:29–36. John the Baptist was a prophet sent by God to prepare the hearts of men for the arrival of their long-awaited Messiah. The next witness is the actual works Jesus performed in his earthly mission. In other words, the works, healings, and miracles solidly prove who he says he is. But in case still more is needed, the third witness is God, who appeared to people like Abraham throughout the Old Testament and told them of the coming Messiah. The fact Jesus fulfilled over 350 Old Testament prophecies[5] given hundreds of years before his birth is no coincidence, but the sovereign fulfillment of God's eternal plan.

Regardless, the Pharisees still resist his claims to be the Messiah. This is why in our passage Jesus points out that if they really understood the Scriptures they study so meticulously, they would see that eternal life is not found in their ability to keep the law but to know and rest in the one who came to abolish it. As we heard from Peter, there is no more sure witness to Jesus than the Scriptures. Even if you heard the audible voice of God, it would not be as certain.

So why do we keep turning to things outside of the Word of God to be our guide or substitute saviors? Jesus is plainly telling us that true life is only found in him—the living Word.

DAY THREE

Straight to My Heart

Before answering the questions, reread the Scripture, being mindful of insights from the first two days.

:: How does each of Jesus's witnesses bear his truth?

:: In John 5:39 what does Jesus mean by saying the Pharisees are looking to find "life" in the Scriptures and not in him?

:: In what ways do you try to secure "life" as the Pharisees did?

DAY FOUR
Back to the Word

:: Reread the Scripture passage and then continue memorizing John 5:39. When you think you know it, write it out below.

:: If Jesus is revealed in the Word and life is only found in him, what can you conclude?

:: What "voices" or "substitute saviors" do you listen to at times to try to process things happening in your life?

DAY FIVE

Journaling and Prayer

:: Write a letter to a friend explaining how it is possible to be sinning even when on the outside we are doing the right things like the Pharisees, acting obediently, and keeping the "law."

Prayer

Lord, help me to see your Word as a testimony to yourself and not simply an instruction book on how to live. Help me find you in them so that I might better believe.

Week 9

All about Him

DAY ONE
Straight from the Word

Read the Scripture and then follow the instructions below.

Note: In this passage two of Jesus's followers are discussing the things that have just happened with Jesus's crucifixion and reports of the empty tomb. They are discouraged because they thought he was the Messiah, but his death dashed their hopes, and it is in their despair that Jesus appears.

:: Luke 24:13–27

[13] That very day two of them were going to a village named Emmaus, about seven miles from Jerusalem, [14] and they were talking with each other about all these things that had happened. [15] While they were talking and discussing together, Jesus himself drew near and went with them. [16] But their eyes were kept from recognizing him. [17] And he said to them, "What is this conversation that you are holding with each other as you walk?" And they stood still, looking sad. [18] Then one of them, named Cleopas, answered him, "Are you the only visitor to Jerusalem who does not know the things that have happened there in these days?" [19] And he said to them, "What things?" And they said to him, "Concerning Jesus of Nazareth, a man who was a prophet mighty in deed and word before God and all the people, [20] and how our chief priests and rulers delivered him up to be condemned to

death, and crucified him. ²¹ But we had hoped that he was the one to redeem Israel. Yes, and besides all this, it is now the third day since these things happened. ²² Moreover, some women of our company amazed us. They were at the tomb early in the morning, ²³ and when they did not find his body, they came back saying that they had even seen a vision of angels, who said that he was alive. ²⁴ Some of those who were with us went to the tomb and found it just as the women had said, but him they did not see." ²⁵ And he said to them, "O foolish ones, and slow of heart to believe all that the prophets have spoken! ²⁶ Was it not necessary that the Christ should suffer these things and enter into his glory?" ²⁷ And beginning with Moses and all the Prophets, he interpreted to them in all the Scriptures the things concerning himself.

:: Underline the primary reason the men walking to the village of Emmaus are sad.

:: Why does Jesus call them foolish?

:: What is Jesus's reason for interpreting the Scriptures for them?

:: If he goes through all the Scriptures, what do you think Jesus is referring to when he says, "beginning with Moses and all the Prophets"?

DAY TWO
The Word Applied

You sit in your hardest class trying to follow the teacher's instruction, but once again feel lost. What makes it worse is the material builds with each lesson, so with every passing class period you fall further behind. The more confused you become, the less motivated you are to even try. Really, you just want the bell to ring to put you out of your misery.

Finally it's time to move to your next class. Though the material is also challenging, the teacher presents the subject in a relatable manner that draws you in and makes remembering it easier.

Now shift from the classroom to imagining yourself on that road to Emmaus walking with your friends, listening to the unknown stranger (you don't realize he is Jesus!) retelling the entire Old Testament. Until now you have always been disinterested in reading it because you didn't understand how it applied to your life and what it all meant. But hearing this man explain it from the beginning, unfolding it in story form, you hear it differently. It suddenly all fits together and makes sense.

This man has just explained how all of the Scriptures from Moses (referencing the first five books of the Bible) through the Prophets (the last seventeen books of the Old Testament) and everything in between are about Jesus! At this time there was no New Testament, so the Scripture Jesus speaks of is solely the Old Testament. These books predate his physical birth and arrival on to the scene, but he has been present for all eternity and is written about on every page.

Do you remember from last week's lesson that Jesus told the Pharisees this same thing?

They prided themselves in their knowledge of the Scriptures, but Jesus said unless they see how they all point to him, then they don't get it all. They misunderstood and misinterpreted what they thought they knew so well.

Likewise, we must view the Scriptures, both the old and the new, with him as the central focus. When we don't, it is like trying to move ahead in that difficult class without understanding the foundation set in the first lessons. We must start with the precept that it is all about him. It is the story of a Redeemer coming for his people to permanently establish his place and rule. This is the foundation that opens our eyes to see what Jesus revealed on the road to Emmaus. Only with that framework can we understand how the rest of the Bible unfolds and builds. And how the Word comes to life in the powerful, life-giving, life-changing person of Jesus.

DAY THREE

Straight to My Heart

Before answering the questions, reread the Scripture, being mindful of insights from the first two days.

:: Why must we see both the Old and New Testaments as one story about Jesus?

:: Why does not seeing Jesus throughout the Bible lead to Pharisaical thoughts and actions?

:: What key verse in this week's reading affirms that the Scripture is all about him?

DAY FOUR
Back to the Word

Reread the Scripture one more time and then take your time answering the questions below.

:: How should viewing the Bible as the unfolding story of Jesus change your focus when you read it?

:: How have you previously approached the Bible more as a rule-book, road map, or self-help book?

:: If the Bible is primarily about him, what does this mean in regard to how you apply it to yourself?

DAY FIVE

Journaling and Prayer

:: Imagine yourself as one of the men traveling to Emmaus when Jesus appeared. What would you ask him to explain from the Bible? What other questions would you have for him? You may consider taking these same questions to your parents, a youth leader, or pastor.

Prayer

Lord, show yourself to me as I read the Word so that I can better understand who you are.

Week 10

Justification Unpacked

DAY ONE

Straight from the Word

Read the Scripture and then follow the instructions below.

Note: This Scripture includes some tough theological words. While short definitions are included in parentheses, greater explanation is given in Day Two: The Word Applied.

:: Romans 3:21–26

[21] But now the righteousness of God has been manifested apart from the law, although the Law and the Prophets bear witness to it— [22] the righteousness of God through faith in Jesus Christ for all who believe. For there is no distinction: [23] for all have sinned and fall short of the glory of God, [24] and are justified [made right] by his grace as a gift, through the redemption that is in Christ Jesus, [25] whom God put forward as a propitiation [atoning sacrifice] by his blood, to be received by faith. This was to show God's righteousness, because in his divine forbearance [patience] he had passed over former sins. [26] It was to show his righteousness at the present time, so that he might be just and the justifier of the one who has faith in Jesus.

:: Romans 4:22–25

22 That is why his [Abraham's] faith was "counted to him as righteous-ness." 23 But the words "it was counted to him" were not written for his sake alone, 24 but for ours also. It will be counted to us who believe in him who raised from the dead Jesus our Lord, 25 who was delivered up for our trespasses [sins] and raised for our justification [setting right by Christ].

:: Circle the repetitive words included in both passages.

:: Underline the difficult-to-understand words along with the given definition.

:: How would you define righteousness?

:: How can righteousness be counted to you?

DAY TWO _____
The Word Applied

Do you skip over verses in the Bible sometimes because you don't know what certain words mean? Perhaps that was even the case yes-terday with the verses in this week's study. Even if you use a modern Bible translation, there are pivotal words in the Christian faith you need to understand. By unpacking the meaning, you will better grasp

Jesus's work on your behalf, so let's break this passage down point by point.

God's standard for righteousness is perfect obedience to the law. For the Jews prior to Jesus's coming, this law includes both the moral law of the Ten Commandments and the ceremonial law pertaining to circumcision, how to prepare food, what animal parts to bring for temple sacrifice, how to build the tabernacle, and many more tedious requirements. This is what the Pharisees worked hard to meticulously uphold.

This same standard of perfection to the moral law is still what we are held to today. A standard that is utterly impossible to ever attain because of our sin nature. How often though we forget this and, like the Pharisees, actually think we are doing good in following all that is required and therefore deserve God's blessing. The reality is we are more sinful than we even know and come nowhere near upholding God's standard of holiness.

Jesus is the only One who kept the law completely and glorifies God perfectly. He is like God and is God in every way and is without sin. He is the only One whose righteous life could serve as the perfect sacrifice that God required. Now for those who believe in him, that righteousness is credited to your account and you are declared righteous! That is what it means to be justified.

Only by God's grace is that possible. Think of grace as God's goodness to the guilty; a gift we did not merit. Our sin, sometimes referred to in the Bible as *trespasses*, declares us guilty and undeserving. But at the cross, Jesus became our "propitiation" or "atoning" sacrifice. In other words, the only way we were made God's friend (reconciled) is because of Jesus's sacrificial death in our place to cover the cost of our sins.

Do you remember in the Garden of Eden when God sacrificed an animal and made skin coverings for Adam and Eve? That was a foretaste of what God provides for you in his Son—his body and blood poured out on your behalf so that his righteousness becomes your covering.

Jesus not only sacrificially died for you, but he lived perfectly for you! So picture King Jesus taking off his robe and putting it around you. Now when God views you he sees the righteous robe of his Son and views you as holy!

DAY THREE

Straight to My Heart

Before answering the questions, reread the Scripture, being mindful of insights from the first two days.

:: What does it mean to be justified?

:: How would you explain the need for "propitiation"?

:: Why is Jesus's perfect life just as necessary as his sacrificial death?

DAY FOUR

Back to the Word

Reread the Scripture one more time and then take your time answering the questions below.

:: What does it mean to have Christ's righteousness?

:: If grace is God's goodness to the guilty, in what ways do you still struggle with thinking that you need to work or perform to earn God's acceptance?

:: How do you see God's grace changing you in the way you relate to your parents and your friends?

DAY FIVE

Journaling and Prayer

:: Over the last weeks, how have the truths of God's Word been impacting you? Have you been challenged? Has your understanding changed or deepened?

Spend time writing your thoughts.

Prayer

Lord, thank you for sending your Son to accomplish in life and in death what was necessary to make me right with you.

Week 11

Perfect Peace

DAY ONE

Straight from the Word

Read the Scripture and then follow the instructions below.

:: **Romans 5:1–2, 18–21**

[1] Therefore, since we have been justified by faith, we have peace with God through our Lord Jesus Christ. [2] Through him we have also obtained access by faith into this grace in which we stand, and we rejoice in hope of the glory of God.

[18] Therefore, as one trespass led to condemnation for all men, so one act of righteousness leads to justification and life for all men. [19] For as by the one man's disobedience the many were made sinners, so by the one man's obedience the many will be made righteous. [20] Now the law came in to increase the trespass, but where sin increased, grace abounded all the more, [21] so that, as sin reigned in death, grace also might reign through righteousness leading to eternal life through Jesus Christ our Lord.

:: **Romans 8:1**

There is therefore now no condemnation for those who are in Christ Jesus.

:: Circle the key words repeated through the verses.

:: Make a list of the words or phrases that relate to justification (e.g., righteousness).

:: Make a list of the words or phrases that relate to trespasses (e.g., condemnation).

:: Underline the verse(s) containing the main idea.

DAY TWO
The Word Applied

When you know you have disappointed your parents and experience their "frown" rather than their "smile," do you feel alone? Do you experience shame? Does it upset you and make you feel unloved? Do you go overboard to please them by being extra helpful and obedient for the next few days until it blows over?

This may be our human experience, but it does not represent God. We don't have to hide, work harder, or do better to earn back his favor. In fact, we can't. There is only one whose work pleased God, and that was Jesus. He did it for us so we can rest in his love.

Jesus lived the perfect life for you and died in your place. His work satisfies God, enabling you to be declared righteous. When you stand on his work—and only his work—God is not going to love you any more when you do better or love you any less when you fail. He remains pleased with you because of Christ.

Do you believe that? Do you believe it even after you have sinned?

As long as you live, you will continue to sin. If you are tracking with me, you may be wondering, *How then can God stay pleased with me?* But what I'm going to say next just shows the sheer radicalness of the gospel. Don't miss this . . .

Your sin, all of it, past, present, and future, is forgiven. Yes, even those sins you haven't committed yet! There is *no* condemnation. Jesus did not come to judge you but to bring peace. Because he satisfied God's wrath for your sin, God views you not as an enemy, but as his holy and righteous child!

Some may think, *Then what difference does it make if I sin?* But the fact that God views you the way he does despite your sin should cause you to fall at his feet in thanksgiving. No longer is sin as appealing because you want to glorify him in all your words, thoughts, and actions. But when you do sin, he will not forsake you, and there is no work required to make up for it. This standing of being deeply loved leads to a greater worship of the one who secured this right standing for you!

You know what else this perspective does? It frees you to admit your sin because you know you are still okay. When you mess up, you don't have to deny it or cover it up. You don't have to pretend to the world that you have it all together.

You can be yourself and rest safely in the arms of your Savior, even when those around you judge and condemn. The quest for rest we've talked about ends in him. You are at peace with God through Jesus.

DAY THREE _____

Straight to My Heart

Before answering the questions, reread the Scripture, being mindful of insights from the first two days.

∷ Why is it hard to believe that God's view of you never changes?

:: How does knowing God loves you change your desires in regard to sin?

:: How does Jesus provide rest and peace for you?

DAY FOUR _____

Back to the Word

Reread the Scripture one more time and then take your time answering the questions below.

:: How should seeing God as a loving Father, rather than a condemning judge, affect you in your sin, your worship, and your understanding of who he is?

:: How might viewing God as a loving Father change the way you treat other people in their sin?

:: Who can you display God's loving-kindness and compassion to? What might that look like?

DAY FIVE _____
Journaling and Prayer

:: Reflect on what it means that you have personally been justified. If you are not sure you have been, use the space to write out a prayer asking God to help you see your need for his perfect life and sacrificial death.

Prayer

Lord, thank you that you came not to condemn but to bring peace. Help me to believe this truth even when I sin.

Week 12

The Only Place to Hide

DAY ONE

Straight from the Word

Read the Scripture and then follow the instructions below.

:: Psalm 32

[1] Blessed is the one whose transgression is forgiven, whose sin is covered.

[2] Blessed is the man against whom the LORD counts no iniquity, and in whose spirit there is no deceit.

[3] For when I kept silent, my bones wasted away through my groaning all day long.

[4] For day and night your hand was heavy upon me; my strength was dried up as by the heat of summer.

[5] I acknowledged my sin to you, and I did not cover my iniquity; I said, "I will confess my transgressions to the LORD," and you forgave the iniquity of my sin.

[6] Therefore let everyone who is godly offer prayer to you at a time when you may be found; surely in the rush of great waters, they shall not reach him.

[7] You are a hiding place for me; you preserve me from trouble; you surround me with shouts of deliverance.

⁸ I will instruct you and teach you in the way you should go; I will counsel you with my eye upon you.

⁹ Be not like a horse or a mule, without understanding, which must be curbed with bit and bridle, or it will not stay near you.

¹⁰ Many are the sorrows of the wicked, but steadfast love surrounds the one who trusts in the LORD.

¹¹ Be glad in the LORD, and rejoice, O righteous, and shout for joy, all you upright in heart!

∷ What is the writer contrasting in this psalm?

∷ Circle the similes and metaphors.

∷ List below what is being described through the similes and metaphors.

∷ Summarize the main idea.

DAY TWO
The Word Applied

Last week we talked about the peace we experience with God through Jesus. What you read in Psalm 32 is King David celebrating this very fact.

For nine months David ran from God, not wanting to expose the sin of his affair with Bathsheba and ordering the murder of her husband Uriah. Of course, God knew. But now David has come clean by humbly confessing his sin to God. And he is overwhelmed by the Lord's unconditional love and forgiveness.

The passage testifies that prior to confessing, David was in physical and emotional torment. He was depressed, empty, restless, and alone. Yet for all that time, his pride kept him from admitting his sin and need for a Savior.

Have there been times you have been like King David trying to hide and cover up your sin? It may be a fabricated story to your parents, covering up what you did over the weekend. It may be the shame of what is really happening when you are alone with your girlfriend or boyfriend. It may be the test you cheated on. It may be the lies to your coach. It may be the food you secretly binge on. It may be the cuts you hide under your sleeves. It may be the pornography on your phone undetected behind an app.

No matter what it is, you either work to convince yourself that what you are doing is justified and not that bad, or you work to suppress the guilt of it because you know what you are doing is wrong and fear forgiveness isn't possible. In either case, you may avoid certain people or busy yourself with activities so you don't have to think about it.

All the while, the secrecy and sin is wreaking havoc in your life, affecting every area including relationships. In your shame you are short with your parents, which leads to arguing and constant conflict. In your secrecy you have withdrawn from your friends who are frustrated by your avoidance and have stopped initiating hang-out time with you. In your guilt you have become defensive. But until you step into the light, there will be no peace. You cannot experience the joy that David expresses in the passage because the only One who can give it has been pushed out.

Once David cried out to the Lord, he found the only solution to his torment and unrest. He found a compassionate, forgiving God who not only removed the sin but also did not hold it against him. A God who did not require David to wallow in guilt or pay penance. David was finally free from the imprisonment he put himself in.

If you feel like David and need help believing your sins are covered and his overwhelming grace and open arms extend to you, I urge you to confide in a parent or seek out a trusted Christian leader, friend, or counselor. Freedom comes in rediscovering what God has already promised—that he is our safe hiding place and deliverer. Running and hiding from God prevents peace from seeping in. Instead run and hide in his unending love for you.

DAY THREE

Straight to My Heart

Before answering the questions, reread the Scripture, being mindful of insights from the first two days.

:: In what ways have you experienced the effects of hiding sin?

:: Why do you still hide your sin and find it hard to confess to God or others?

:: How would life be different if you ran to God as your hiding place instead of hiding from him?

DAY FOUR
Back to the Word

Reread the Scripture one more time and then take your time answering the questions below.

:: David is overwhelmed with the reality that God could forgive him. What truth must you believe to experience this same joy?

:: According to Psalm 32, how does God view you when you sin?

:: Is it hard for you to believe God doesn't keep a record of your sin? Why or why not?

DAY FIVE

Journaling and Prayer

:: Write about a time when you were afraid to confess to God or to someone else. How did that burden take a toll on you? What did it feel like once you came clean? If you need to confess something now, write about what you are feeling and what is holding you back. Ask God to help you act.

If you are struggling with a more serious issue or addiction, please ask God for the courage to confide in your parents, Christian leader, counselor, or other adult. May God fill you with his peace in taking that first step to getting the help you need and may he help you to believe that in him there is always hope for change.

Prayer

Lord, you are my safe haven. Help me not doubt that you want me to come to you even in my sin.

Week 13

Unquenchable Thirst

DAY ONE

Straight from the Word

Read the Scripture and then follow the instructions below.

:: John 4:5–7, 9–29

[5] So he [Jesus] came to a town of Samaria. . . . [6] Jacob's well was there; so Jesus, wearied as he was from his journey, was sitting beside the well. It was about the sixth hour. [7] A woman from Samaria came to draw water. Jesus said to her, "Give me a drink."

[9] The Samaritan woman said to him, "How is it that you, a Jew, ask for a drink from me, a woman of Samaria?" (For Jews have no dealings with Samaritans.) [10] Jesus answered her, "If you knew the gift of God, and who it is that is saying to you, 'Give me a drink,' you would have asked him, and he would have given you living water." [11] The woman said to him, "Sir, you have nothing to draw water with, and the well is deep. Where do you get that living water? . . . [13] Jesus said to her, "Everyone who drinks of this water will be thirsty again, [14] but whoever drinks of the water that I will give him will never be thirsty again. The water that I will give him will become in him a spring of water welling up to eternal life." [15] The woman said to him, "Sir, give me this water, so that I will not be thirsty or have to come here to draw water."

[16] Jesus said to her, "Go, call your husband, and come here." [17] The woman answered him, "I have no husband." Jesus said to her, "You are right in saying, 'I have no husband'; [18] for you have had five husbands, and the one you now have is not your husband. What you have said is true." [21] Jesus said to her, "Woman, . . ." [22] You worship what you do not know; we worship what we know, for salvation is from the Jews. [23] But the hour is coming, and is now here, when the true worshipers will worship the Father in spirit and truth, for the Father is seeking such people to worship him. . . ." [25] The woman said to him, "I know that Messiah is coming (he who is called Christ). When he comes he will tell us all things." [26] Jesus said to her, "I who speak to you am he." [28] . . . So the woman left her water jar and went away into town and said to the people, [29]"Come, see a man who told me all that I ever did. Can this be the Christ?"

:: Make five observations about the woman.

:: Circle all the words related to and including "water."

:: What significance do you see in the use of these words?

:: Write down any thoughts or questions.

DAY TWO
The Word Applied

I am a runner. Four times I have gone through the crazy training regimen necessary to complete marathons, and each time on at least one of my long training runs I have wondered *Why I am doing this again!* To be race-day ready the training has to be treated like a job, which means getting the long miles in regardless of the weather—freezing cold, tornado-like winds, or extreme heat. With each passing week, mileage is increased to build strength and endurance. Along with that is the need to stay properly hydrated, which mean getting enough water before your body actually needs it. Otherwise, it may be too late to recover from dehydration.

Unfortunately, this happened to me in one race. I crossed the finish line and nearly fainted as I was quickly taken to the medical tent. My blood pressure dipped dangerously, and the medics determined I was dehydrated. I had neglected to realize how desperately I needed thirst quenching.

This week John introduces us to the Samaritan woman who has come to draw water in the heat of the day. At the well she encounters Jesus. When he mentions "living water," she perks up, thinking how nice it would be not to need more water or to make the daily trek to the well. But she does not initially understand that Jesus is talking about a different kind of water and a much deeper thirst.

When Jesus says, "Go call your husband," knowing she does not have a husband, he draws attention to the fact that she is looking to men to fill her longing and thirst to be loved. Her desire to be loved is not wrong; what's wrong is where she tries to satisfy that thirst. She is turning to something other than God to give her the love that only he can give. For her, men have taken God's rightful place in her heart, and she believes they will give her what she thirsts after.

Like the Samaritan woman or like me becoming dehydrated, we fail to realize how deep our thirst is to be loved, accepted, and secure. We chase after things (idols) that we think will bring satisfaction and life, only to realize we still aren't filled. We grow more and more depleted, discontent, and desperate in the ways we try to quench those desires.

What stands out in this story is that when Jesus exposed the sin and need of the Samaritan woman, he did not condemn her, but pursued her. He looked upon her with compassion, giving grace and mercy even in her sin. At the end of the text she left behind her water jug, signifying that after drinking of the "Living Water" he offers, she no longer needed to look elsewhere to be filled. Her thirst had been quenched.

Go draw from the source of "Living Water" and be filled!

DAY THREE

Straight to My Heart

Before answering the questions, reread the Scripture, being mindful of insights from the first two days.

:: What is our deepest thirst?

:: What does the Samaritan woman's left-behind jug symbolize?

:: What are some of the idols you seek after to quench your thirst?

DAY FOUR

Back to the Word

Reread the Scripture one more time and then take your time answering the questions below.

:: How is Jesus as the "Living Water" the answer to permanently quenching your "thirst"?

:: What thirsts do you see in the lives of your friends?

:: How might God use you to see their thirst and point them to the "Living Water"?

DAY FIVE

Journaling and Prayer

:: Though you may see Jesus's love as the "Living Water" that quenches your thirsts, your heart will still turn to idols. How can understanding justification help you return to Jesus and repent more quickly?

Write out your thoughts.

Prayer

Lord, I look to all sorts of false gods to quench my thirst. Help me know you as the source of "Living Water" and only means to permanently fill me.

Week 14

Debt Free

DAY ONE

Straight from the Word

Read the Scripture and then follow the instructions below.

:: John 13:1–17, 36–38

[1] Now before the Feast of the Passover, when Jesus knew that his hour had come to depart out of this world to the Father, having loved his own who were in the world, he loved them to the end. [2] During supper, when the devil had already put it into the heart of Judas Iscariot, Simon's son, to betray him, [3] Jesus, knowing that the Father had given all things into his hands, and that he had come from God and was going back to God, [4] rose from supper. He laid aside his outer garments, and taking a towel, tied it around his waist. [5] Then he poured water into a basin and began to wash the disciples' feet and to wipe them with the towel that was wrapped around him. [6] He came to Simon Peter, who said to him, "Lord, do you wash my feet?" [7] Jesus answered him, "What I am doing you do not understand now, but afterward you will understand." [8] Peter said to him, "You shall never wash my feet." Jesus answered him, "If I do not wash you, you have no share with me." [9] Simon Peter said to him, "Lord, not my feet only but also my hands and my head!" [10] Jesus said to him, "The one who has bathed does not need to wash, except for his feet, but is completely clean. And you are clean, but not every one of

you." [11] For he knew who was to betray him; that was why he said, "Not all of you are clean."

[12] When he had washed their feet and put on his outer garments and resumed his place, he said to them, "Do you understand what I have done to you? [13] You call me Teacher and Lord, and you are right, for so I am. [14] If I then, your Lord and Teacher, have washed your feet, you also ought to wash one another's feet. [15] For I have given you an example, that you also should do just as I have done to you. [16] Truly, truly, I say to you, a servant is not greater than his master, nor is a messenger greater than the one who sent him. [17] If you know these things, blessed are you if you do them. . . ."

[36] Simon Peter said to him, "Lord, where are you going?" Jesus answered him, "Where I am going you cannot follow me now, but you will follow afterward." [37] Peter said to him, "Lord, why can I not follow you now? I will lay down my life for you." [38] Jesus answered, "Will you lay down your life for me? Truly, truly, I say to you, the rooster will not crow till you have denied me three times."

:: Underline the words or phrases indicating the setting, such as time or location.

:: Make five observations about Peter from his dialogue with Jesus.

:: Write down your thoughts as to the timing of when Jesus washed their feet.

:: What are the disciples being called to do?

DAY TWO

The Word Applied

Have you ever been out to dinner with friends and not realized until the check came you were short on cash? Did you feel guilt or shame over one of them having to cover for you, even if they were happy to help? What about if someone gives you frequent rides or helps you out with something you are dreading—do you feel like you owe them gas money or must return the favor? Is it hard to freely accept a gift?

Sadly, many Christians live their lives as if they have to repay Jesus for his sacrifice. This may not be what we say we believe, but in reality that is how we live. We think we have to be worthy to receive God's love. Jesus's washing his disciples' feet stretches our comprehension of grace by showing us just how far he will stoop to display his love for us.

In the days of Jesus, no Jew ate a special meal without first having his feet washed. It was a job performed by the lowest servant of the house. But on the night Jesus was celebrating the Passover meal in a rented room with his disciples, there was not a servant present to wash feet. So Jesus got up to do it himself.

This act of service is much more than an example for us to follow! The greater significance is seen in Peter's response. Peter's struggle to allow Jesus to wash his feet is really his struggle to receive the Lord's grace. Peter feels like he doesn't deserve it or isn't worthy to receive it. He doesn't understand Jesus's grace at this point. But, Peter will.

Not until after, though. After denying three times any association and friendship with Jesus and then having to wrestle with the guilt and shame of those denials. After watching Jesus suffer and die for him. After Jesus rises from the grave—THEN Peter will understand his need for the cleansing job that Jesus humbly performed for him.

Do you understand what he has done for you?

Jesus lays aside his rights as God and humbly takes on the form of a servant to serve you by dying in your place in order to wash away the filth of your sin. The One who has authority over all things rises up from supper, lays aside his clothes, grabs a towel, and proceeds to stoop down to wash his disciples' dirty, sweaty, smelly feet!

Why does Jesus do this?

John 13:1 tells us that Jesus "having loved his own who were in the world, he loved them to the end." Jesus knew Peter (and all others) would deny, desert, and forsake him, yet "he loved them to the end"!

This means he loves you to the end of his strength and beyond. He loves you to the end of ALL of your failures, backsliding, selfishness, unworthiness, and ALL of your sin. Jesus's washing his disciples' feet shows you that his love for his people has no limits. To death he went to free you of the debt of sin!

DAY THREE

Straight to My Heart

Before answering the questions, reread the Scripture, being mindful of insights from the first two days.

:: Why is it hard for you to accept that Jesus freely gives grace?

:: What are ways you try to make yourself worthy to be loved by Jesus?

:: How does Jesus's washing his disciples feet show what he came to do?

DAY FOUR
Back to the Word

Reread the Scripture one more time and then take your time answering the questions below.

:: How does understanding this passage challenge you in the way you love others?

:: Considering how hard it is to love others when they sin against you, how does this expand your comprehension for what Jesus did?

:: In what way have you been challenged to reach out to someone today?

DAY FIVE
Journaling and Prayer

:: If you are familiar with the children's story *Guess How Much I Love You*, you may recall the father rabbit telling his son, "I love you right up to the moon—and back."[6] Reflect on this concept of immeasurable love as the love of Jesus for you.

Prayer

Lord, thank you for not requiring I make myself worthy of your love. Because of this truth, give me the grace to love others regardless of whether or not they deserve it.

Week 15

Always on His Mind

DAY ONE
Straight from the Word

Read the Scripture and then follow the instructions below.

*Note: In John 14–16 Jesus is preparing his disciples for his depar-
ture, and now in John 17 he wants them to hear what is in his heart as
he prays to the Father. The Genesis passage precedes the John 17 verses
because Jesus accomplishes what Adam failed to do.*

:: Genesis 2:9, 15–17

[9] And out of the ground the LORD God made to spring up every tree
that is pleasant to the sight and good for food. The tree of life was in the
midst of the garden, and the tree of the knowledge of good and evil. . . .
[15] The LORD God took the man and put him in the garden of Eden to
work it and keep it. [16] And the LORD God commanded the man, saying, "You may surely eat of every tree of the garden, [17] but of the tree
of the knowledge of good and evil you shall not eat, for in the day that
you eat of it you shall surely die."

:: John 17:1–5

[1] When Jesus had spoken these words, he lifted up his eyes to heaven,
and said, "Father, the hour has come; glorify your Son that the Son
may glorify you, [2] since you have given him authority over all flesh, to
give eternal life to all whom you have given him. [3] And this is eternal

life, that they know you the only true God, and Jesus Christ whom you have sent. ⁴ I glorified you on earth, having accomplished the work that you gave me to do. ⁵ And now, Father, glorify me in your own presence with the glory that I had with you before the world existed."

:: What is the work God gave Adam and Eve? Was it accomplished?

:: What is the work God gave Jesus? Was it accomplished?

:: Underline the explanation of how one gains eternal life.
:: Whose work merits eternal life?

DAY TWO

The Word Applied

When someone prays out loud, it's like a window to the heart. You hear the emotion and the passion of what is inside them, which leads to knowing that person better. This is what happens in John 17 when we are privy to Jesus's prayer to the Father just before he is arrested.

This prayer, known as his high priestly prayer, gives us a glimpse into the conversation between the Trinity before the creation of the world! Jesus is talking to God about that eternal plan discussed between them before time. Before they created the heavens and the earth. Before God made man in his own image, crowning him with glory. Before God gave Adam and Eve dominion over all that he had made.

Before all this, God knew that Adam would rebel against him and trust Satan's word over his word. He knew that in pride Adam would seek to exalt his own glory over the glory of the God who made him. God knew Adam would spurn his love, throwing off God's rule in attempt to be his own king ruling his own life.

God knew that Adam's sin would bring death into the world, affecting all he had made. But, God also had an eternal plan to deal with Adam's sin and to save man from sin's punishment. Jesus's prayer reveals this. In this prayer we hear that salvation through Jesus was God's idea for this eternal plan. That means God is for YOU!

Do you live like this is true?

We tend to think instead that God is opposed to us. We think we have to walk on eggshells to pacify his anger and do good things to appease him. And then we think we need Jesus to plead with God on our behalf to have pity on us. But that is not the case!

Jesus's prayer proves this thinking false because it is God who planned and purposed his people's salvation. Our sin doesn't catch him off guard. There is nothing accidental about the plan and nothing to be modified. Before sin entered the world, God had a perfect plan about how to deal with sin in order to save us.

So what does that mean for the Christian?

It means that you were the object of God's interest and concern before the foundation of the world! From all eternity you have been on the mind and heart of God. And Jesus agreed to carry out and accomplish that plan.

By praying this prayer, Jesus wants his disciples who hear it, and you and me, to know we always will be and always have been on his mind. Like Adam, even in our sin, we can rest knowing our salvation is secure by the life, death, and resurrection of God's obedient Son.

DAY THREE _____

Straight to My Heart

Before answering the questions, reread the Scripture, being mindful of insights from the first two days.

:: What makes you feel like God is against you and not for you?

:: What truths about God do you see more clearly?

:: How is Jesus's prayer a comfort to you?

DAY FOUR _____

Back to the Word

Reread the Scripture one more time and then take your time answering the questions below.

:: In your words, tell about the conversation taking place between the Father and the Son.

:: Jesus prayed, "Glorify your Son that your Son may glorify you." How do you think each were glorified?

:: How do you think you glorify God?

DAY FIVE

Journaling and Prayer

:: Do you know what it is like to have something always on your mind? Now consider that YOU were and are always on God's mind. Write about how this makes you feel.

Prayer

Lord, help me believe there is nothing I can do to change or add to make my salvation more complete. Thank you that I am secure in you.

Week 16

Slaves Set Free

DAY ONE
Straight from the Word

Read the Scripture and then follow the instructions below.

:: Exodus 1:1–14

[1] These are the names of the sons of Israel who came to Egypt with Jacob, each with his household: [2] Reuben, Simeon, Levi, and Judah, [3] Issachar, Zebulun, and Benjamin, [4] Dan and Naphtali, Gad and Asher. [5] All the descendants of Jacob were seventy persons; Joseph was already in Egypt. [6] Then Joseph died, and all his brothers and all that generation. [7] But the people of Israel were fruitful and increased greatly; they multiplied and grew exceedingly strong, so that the land was filled with them. [8] Now there arose a new king over Egypt, who did not know Joseph. [9] And he said to his people, "Behold, the people of Israel are too many and too mighty for us. [10] Come, let us deal shrewdly with them, lest they multiply, and, if war breaks out, they join our enemies and fight against us and escape from the land." [11] Therefore they set taskmasters over them to afflict them with heavy burdens. They built for Pharaoh store cities, Pithom and Raamses. [12] But the more they were oppressed, the more they multiplied and the more they spread abroad. And the Egyptians were in dread of the people of Israel. [13] So they ruthlessly made the people of Israel work as slaves [14] and

made their lives bitter with hard service, in mortar and brick, and in all kinds of work in the field. In all their work they ruthlessly made them work as slaves.

:: Exodus 2:23–25

23 During those many days the king of Egypt died, and the people of Israel groaned because of their slavery and cried out for help. Their cry for rescue from slavery came up to God. 24 And God heard their groaning, and God remembered his covenant with Abraham, with Isaac, and with Jacob. 25 God saw the people of Israel—and God knew.

:: Make five observations from the passages.

:: What is the primary reason the Egyptians dreaded the Israelites?

:: Circle the action verbs ascribed to God.

:: Write down any thoughts or questions.

DAY TWO

The Word Applied

This Exodus scene shows us what life is like living under the wrong ruler, in the wrong kingdom. What we notice from the passage is it is a life of slavery and death. This is a picture of sin's rule over our lives. Just like with the oppressive Egyptian taskmasters over the Israelites, sin seeks to enslave in order to destroy us. Life outside of God's kingdom where he reigns over our hearts is bondage.

Let's think about this in terms of something you should identify with to some degree or another: the desire for acceptance, approval, and love from others. While initially the desire may not be sinful, what happens when you don't get what you want? Do you try harder to please, to control, or to manipulate to get the right response from another person or group?

This desire may play out in your motivation behind making the best grades or joining certain school clubs. You think if you perform at a certain level or are associated with certain things, then your parents, teachers, or peers will think more highly of you. Same thing in sports, in the arts, in jobs—we want to be the best, to be noticed, to receive recognition from others. And if the compliments and attention don't come, you either work harder or fall apart under the weight of trying to live up to perfection. In the process you may gossip or slander those you view as your competition. Or you may constantly talk about yourself, making your accomplishments known, as you seek affirmation for how "great" you are.

On social media, you may post for the sole purpose of being re-tweeted or "liked." You strive to accumulate hundreds, even thousands, of "friends," all in an effort to portray to the world that you are witty, beautiful, important, or influential. However, in order to maintain that image, you have to continue coming up with the best post and prettiest pictures. That takes work, and without realizing it you become enslaved to the desire of wanting others' approval.

Do you see how enslaving these desires are in the way they control your thoughts and actions? This is bondage. This is what life is like living under the wrong ruler. Without even realizing it, you have become a slave to the powerful pull of sin.

To recognize it for what it is and then to cry out for help is a good thing! Just as God heard the cry of the Israelites in the anguish of their slavery and did something about it (Exodus 2:23–25), he hears you. This is the reason he rejected his own Son's prayer and allowed him to die on the cross so he could answer *your* cry and be your Rescuer, setting you free from the bondage and penalty of sin.

DAY THREE

Straight to My Heart

Before answering the questions, reread the Scripture, being mindful of insights from the first two days.

:: In your life, how have you seen sin to be oppressive and enslaving?

:: "God heard their cry for rescue from slavery and did something about it" sums up the big idea of the passage. What does this tell us?

:: How does freedom from the bondage of sin affirm last week's lesson summary—that you have always been on his mind?

DAY FOUR   _____

Back to the Word

Reread the Scripture one more time and then take your time answering the questions below.

:: Even though you may still be clinging to or enslaved by a specific sin, how would remembering God's steadfast love give you strength to confess and turn away from that sin?

:: When you commit the same sin next time, what do you need to remember again?

:: If he is safe to go to in your sin, what does this tell you about how we should treat others in their sin?

DAY FIVE   _____

Journaling and Prayer

:: Considering how God treated the Israelites in their enslavement and also how he treats you in your enslaving sin, what do you see about his character? Include in your journal entry other attributes of God and how this is comforting to you.

Prayer

Lord, thank you for faithfully loving me even though I continue to fall back into sin's trap. Help me to see it as enslaving bondage.

Week 17

Righteous Robes

DAY ONE
Straight from the Word
Read the Scripture and then follow the instructions below.

:: John 19:17–18, 23–37

[17] And he [Jesus] went out, bearing his own cross, to the place called The Place of a Skull, which in Aramaic is called Golgotha. [18] There they crucified him, and with him two others, one on either side, and Jesus between them.

[23] When the soldiers had crucified Jesus, they took his garments and divided them into four parts, one part for each soldier; also his tunic. But the tunic was seamless, woven in one piece from top to bottom, [24] so they said to one another, "Let us not tear it, but cast lots for it to see whose it shall be." This was to fulfill the Scripture which says, "They divided my garments among them, and for my clothing they cast lots." So the soldiers did these things, [25] but standing by the cross of Jesus were his mother and his mother's sister, Mary the wife of Clopas, and Mary Magdalene. [26] When Jesus saw his mother and the disciple whom he loved standing nearby, he said to his mother, "Woman, behold, your son!" [27] Then he said to the disciple, "Behold, your mother!" And from that hour the disciple took her to his own home.

[28] After this, Jesus, knowing that all was now finished, said (to fulfill the Scripture), "I thirst." [29] A jar full of sour wine stood there, so they put a sponge full of the sour wine on a hyssop branch and held it to his mouth. [30] When Jesus had received the sour wine, he said, "It is finished," and he bowed his head and gave up his spirit.

[31] Since it was the day of Preparation, and so that the bodies would not remain on the cross on the Sabbath (for that Sabbath was a high day), the Jews asked Pilate that their legs might be broken and that they might be taken away. [32] So the soldiers came and broke the legs of the first, and of the other who had been crucified with him. [33] But when they came to Jesus and saw that he was already dead, they did not break his legs. [34] But one of the soldiers pierced his side with a spear, and at once there came out blood and water. [35] He who saw it has borne witness—his testimony is true, and he knows that he is telling the truth—that you also may believe. [36] For these things took place that the Scripture might be fulfilled: "Not one of his bones will be broken." [37] And again another Scripture says, "They will look on him whom they have pierced."

:: Make five observations from the passage about Jesus.

:: Why do you think Jesus had to go thirsty?

:: Underline everything mentioned as fulfilling of the Scripture.

:: What is the significance of Jesus's last words, "It is finished"?

DAY TWO

The Word Applied

Have you ever been completely humiliated in public? You feel your face flush and you can't escape fast enough. What if you then learn your friends captured the embarrassing moment on their phones and sent it viral? It feels like the whole world is laughing at you, and your friends have no regard for how that makes you feel.

Now imagine Jesus experiencing utter rejection from those he came to save. There he was, fully God, being put to death because people did not believe him to be who he knew he was. But as fully man that means he felt every bit of the excruciating pain of the leather straps whipping his back and the nails driven into his hands and feet. It also means he felt the humiliation of being stripped of his clothes and hung naked on the cross for anyone to gawk at.

Public exposure in this vulnerable and defenseless state was part of the punishment in Roman crucifixion. Worse than being left unprotected to the elements is the shame of being unable to control what people see.

Nakedness always refers to shame except one place in the Bible— in the garden before Adam and Eve sinned and were said to be "naked and unashamed" with nothing to hide or cover up. There was no fear in being totally exposed, no fear of being rejected, no fear of someone seeing them as they really were.

We experience shame because of sin. So we cover up, and we try to control how God and others see us. We fear that if God sees who we really are, he will reject us. And if other people knew what we know, they would reject us too.

But here is the good news: Jesus experienced that nakedness on the cross in order to cover your shame. He was naked and put to shame so that you could be completely covered in his righteousness. Therefore, God *does not* look at you with condemnation.

Understanding the implications of this is freedom. It means you can stop hiding. You do not need to try to control how God and others see you. You do not have to fear approaching God in your sin. You can be open and honest without questioning his acceptance of you.

Do you believe this? Do you believe that even if you are covering something up now you can go to God with it?

Remember the Samaritan woman at the well? God looked at her in her sin with compassion and that is exactly the same way he looks at you. So lay the "fig leaves" aside because you have a greater covering—the perfect covering. You stand fully clothed in the righteous robes of the King!

DAY THREE _____

Straight to My Heart

Before answering the questions, reread the Scripture, being mindful of insights from the first two days.

:: How does thinking about Jesus being fully man experiencing humiliation, pain, and shame help you grasp the full weight of the cross?

:: In your words, write what Jesus's nakedness and shame did for you.

:: What shame or sin have you been carrying that you feel like you have to keep hidden?

DAY FOUR   _____
Back to the Word

Reread the Scripture one more time and then take your time answering the questions below.

:: If your shame was covered at the cross, how should this free you to live differently?

:: How would living free affect the degree to which you are concerned about other's opinions and view of you?

:: How can freedom from living under the weight of shame and condemnation spur you toward others?

DAY FIVE

Journaling and Prayer

:: If Christ's righteous robes are covering you, how does he view you? Tell about how this changes or deepens your understanding of him?

Prayer

Lord, thank you for enduring the shame of the cross for me. Free me from the condemnation I often feel and help me to know your look of love is on me.

Week 18

Behold Him

DAY ONE

Straight from the Word

Read the Scripture and then follow the instructions below.

:: 2 Corinthians 3:1–18

[1] Are we beginning to commend ourselves again? Or do we need, as some do, letters of recommendation to you, or from you? [2] You yourselves are our letter of recommendation, written on our hearts, to be known and read by all. [3] And you show that you are a letter from Christ delivered by us, written not with ink but with the Spirit of the living God, not on tablets of stone but on tablets of human hearts.

[4] Such is the confidence that we have through Christ toward God. [5] Not that we are sufficient in ourselves to claim anything as coming from us, but our sufficiency is from God, [6] who has made us sufficient to be ministers of a new covenant, not of the letter but of the Spirit. For the letter kills, but the Spirit gives life.

[7] Now if the ministry of death, carved in letters on stone, came with such glory that the Israelites could not gaze at Moses' face because of its glory, which was being brought to an end, [8] will not the ministry of the Spirit have even more glory? [9] For if there was glory in the ministry of condemnation, the ministry of righteousness must far exceed it in glory. [10] Indeed, in this case, what once had glory has come to have no glory

at all, because of the glory that surpasses it. [11] For if what was being brought to an end came with glory, much more will what is permanent have glory.

[12] Since we have such a hope, we are very bold, [13] not like Moses, who would put a veil over his face so that the Israelites might not gaze at the outcome of what was being brought to an end. [14] But their minds were hardened. For to this day, when they read the old covenant, that same veil remains unlifted, because only through Christ is it taken away. [15] Yes, to this day whenever Moses is read a veil lies over their hearts. [16] But when one turns to the Lord, the veil is removed. [17] Now the Lord is the Spirit, and where the Spirit of the Lord is, there is freedom. [18] And we all, with unveiled face, beholding the glory of the Lord, are being transformed into the same image from one degree of glory to another. For this comes from the Lord who is the Spirit.

∷ Circle the repetitive key words in the passage.

∷ What is the glory of Christ being contrasted to?

∷ What makes the Spirit's ministry more glorious than the old covenant?

∷ Underline how the veil is removed.

DAY TWO
The Word Applied

Have you taken off the glasses in a 3-D movie to see what the picture looks like? What you see is blurry, and you miss the effect of things jumping off the screen. The fuzzy view conceals the details, preventing you from seeing it as designed. Similarly, 2 Corinthians 3:18 states that when we see God clearly and the veil is removed, we will gaze upon the perfect picture of what we are supposed to see.

So what is that perfect picture? How do we know if God's full glory is being distorted or if we are seeing clearly?

Each week this book has been pointing you to Jesus. As we talked about in the beginning, that is because the Bible is his story and you must know what that story is. If you focus on yourself without knowing who he is—why he is necessary and who he is for you—then his glory will fade in your life. But when you see all of who Jesus is, his glory will begin to transform your life.

In our passage we are told that transformation happens when you "behold" him. By looking at him, the Spirit changes you to begin to look more like him. This may surprise you, but being transformed into his likeness does not mean that you become less and less sinful. No, it means that as you see more and more of your sin, you see your great need for a Savior. And in seeing your need, you are being sanctified.

This word "sanctified" or "sanctification" means being made holy, growing in grace or being transformed to be more like him. It is the steady state of existence we remain in after we are "justified"— that is, being declared righteous—and before we are "glorified"— when we are risen with Christ to heaven. It is a lifelong process for the believer; you cannot view it as a level of spirituality you will arrive at after a certain amount of time or hard work. It is an act of the Holy Spirit. Your job is to behold Christ.

To stay focused on who he is and what he did for you means that you never graduate from the gospel. You don't "accept" Christ and then move on to something else to be sanctified. You must constantly hear the gospel. If instead you think you have that down, but now you need "ten steps to holy living" or "three points to help you stop sinning," then you are turning to your own work and away from Christ's work. The transformation of growing in grace happens in understanding his story; resting in his finished work for you and remembering you have on his righteous robes.

Behold him by keeping your eyes on him, depending on him, trusting him, and believing in him—not yourself!

DAY THREE _____

Straight to My Heart

Before answering the questions, reread the Scripture, being mindful of insights from the first two days.

:: What is the definition of *sanctification*?

:: What keeps you from seeing Christ with an unveiled face?

:: Why is the gospel crucial not just for being saved, but also growing as a Christian?

DAY FOUR _____
Back to the Word

Reread the Scripture one more time and then take your time answering the questions below.

:: If the Spirit is transforming you more into his image as you behold him, what does it look like for you to behold him?

:: Why is simply beholding him so challenging?

:: Even when beholding him is difficult, what is the confidence you have in Christ?

DAY FIVE

Journaling and Prayer

:: We have reached the end of Part I: Getting the Story Straight. Reflect on what the Lord has revealed to you over the past eighteen weeks. How have you grown? What are you struggling with?

Spend time writing out your thoughts.

Prayer

Lord, help me grow in grace by focusing on your righteousness for me, not my own performance or good works.

PART II

My Life Mixed into the Story

Scripture Memory:

For freedom Christ has set us free;
stand firm therefore, and do not submit
again to a yoke of slavery.
(Galatians 5:1)

Week 19

Hope to Hold on To

DAY ONE
Straight from the Word
Read the Scripture and then follow the instructions below.

:: Romans 5:1–11

[1] Therefore, since we have been justified by faith, we have peace with God through our Lord Jesus Christ. [2] Through him we have also obtained access by faith into this grace in which we stand, and we rejoice in hope of the glory of God. [3] Not only that, but we rejoice in our sufferings, knowing that suffering produces endurance, [4] and endurance produces character, and character produces hope, [5] and hope does not put us to shame, because God's love has been poured into our hearts through the Holy Spirit who has been given to us. [6] For while we were still weak, at the right time Christ died for the ungodly. [7] For one will scarcely die for a righteous person—though perhaps for a good person one would dare even to die— [8] but God shows his love for us in that while we were still sinners, Christ died for us. [9] Since, therefore, we have now been justified by his blood, much more shall we be saved by him from the wrath of God. [10] For if while we were enemies we were reconciled to God by the death of his Son, much more, now that we are reconciled, shall we be saved by his life. [11] More than that, we also

rejoice in God through our Lord Jesus Christ, through whom we have now received reconciliation.

:: Underline everything obtained through justification.

:: How are we reconciled to God?

:: What is amazing about who Christ dies for and why?

:: Write down any thoughts or questions.

DAY TWO

The Word Applied

Do you ever fear that God at some point will stop forgiving you when you sin? Do you doubt that he really views you as righteous when you continue to sin? Do you struggle to believe you are really growing in Christlikeness?

Even for the believer, sin's nature and Satan's goal never change. Like a magnetic force pulling you away from God, it will continue seeking to destroy. And that powerful remaining presence is what causes your questions and doubts. Even though sin's penalty has been paid once and for all, it is still easy to feel insecure about God's love when you keep sinning. Knowing that your struggle with sin can make you feel this way, Paul wrote Romans 5 to strengthen your hope in God by driving home the point that your standing before him is not based on how hard you hold to God but his mighty hold on you!

Look back at verses 1–2. "Having been justified" is a completed past action done by God in the one-time act when you were declared righteous before him. Verse 9 goes on to say, "Much more then, having now been justified by his blood [again past action], we shall be saved [in the future] from God's wrath through Christ." Christ's blood is the basis for God declaring you righteous NOW, and it is the basis for being declared righteous on that future Day of Judgment.

That is not all. According to verse 10, when were you united to God? When you were God's enemy! So if you were reconciled when you were an enemy, how much more certain can you be of your salvation now that you are God's child and friend?

Do you see the logic?

God didn't pour out his wrath on you when you were his enemy, instead he poured out his wrath on his Son in order to make you his friend. And now that you are friends, God will work to keep you a friend. The basis for your present and future hope of the glory of God proceeds from Christ's accomplished work in the past on the cross. This means that the only way God will deal with his friends is according to grace!

When you sin, there is no wrath, just grace. When you commit the same sin for the thousandth time—grace. When you hurt someone else because of your sin—grace. When you're angry with God—grace. When you doubt God—grace. When you hurt and suffer—grace. When you can't forgive yourself or others—grace. When you lack faith—grace.

The hope that Paul wants you to hold on to when sin seeks to pull you away from God is not your hold on God. Trust in the security and strength of God's hold on you, his friend!

DAY THREE

Straight to My Heart

Before answering the questions, reread the Scripture, being mindful of insights from the first two days.

:: Why do you doubt God's love for you when you sin?

:: How does this passage speak to those doubts with assurance of your standing before him?

:: How does it make you feel to know God calls you his friend despite anything you have done?

DAY FOUR

Back to the Word

Reread the Scripture one more time and then take your time answering the questions below.

:: Why is hope found in God's hold on you, and not how well you hold on to him?

:: How do you live or not live according to this belief?

:: Why do you think many Christians struggle to believe this is true?

DAY FIVE

Journaling and Prayer

:: Reread the end of the devotional on Day 2 about his amazing grace, and write about what grace like this means for you. Can you even comprehend it?

Prayer

Lord, thank you for your eternal hold on me. Help me when my sin causes me to doubt that nothing disqualifies me or changes your love for me.

Week 20

The Second Adam Succeeds

DAY ONE
Straight from the Word

Read the Scripture and then follow the instructions below.

:: Romans 5:12–21

[12] Therefore, just as sin came into the world through one man, and death through sin, and so death spread to all men because all sinned—[13] for sin indeed was in the world before the law was given, but sin is not counted where there is no law. [14] Yet death reigned from Adam to Moses, even over those whose sinning was not like the transgression of Adam, who was a type of the one who was to come.

[15] But the free gift is not like the trespass. For if many died through one man's trespass, much more have the grace of God and the free gift by the grace of that one man Jesus Christ abounded for many. [16] And the free gift is not like the result of that one man's sin. For the judgment following one trespass brought condemnation, but the free gift following many trespasses brought justification. [17] For if, because of one man's trespass, death reigned through that one man, much more will those who receive the abundance of grace and the free gift of righteousness reign in life through the one man Jesus Christ.

¹⁸ Therefore, as one trespass led to condemnation for all men, so one act of righteousness leads to justification and life for all men. ¹⁹ For as by the one man's disobedience the many were made sinners, so by the one man's obedience the many will be made righteous. ²⁰ Now the law came in to increase the trespass, but where sin increased, grace abounded all the more, ²¹ so that, as sin reigned in death, grace also might reign through righteousness leading to eternal life through Jesus Christ our Lord.

:: Circle the repetitive key words.

:: Make two columns: one showing the work of Adam and one the work of Christ.

:: What are the contrasts between Adam's work and Christ's work?

:: What confuses you in these verses?

DAY TWO

The Word Applied

If you are like me, this passage is hard to follow and would be easy to skip over. But the implications of it are important to understand, so stick with me as I break it down to the core.

We have Adam and we have God. And we have the issue of identity. As seen in past weeks, Adam was created by God to bear his image in the world. Man has an elevated status and special relationship to God. But when Adam sinned, that sin nature was spread to all mankind for all time. Never again would man be righteous on his own accord.

Enter Christ here. Jesus represents a second Adam. As we've previously discussed, this is not God having to come up with a new plan because the first one didn't work out. But according to his eternal plan, Christ incarnate would come to live the righteous life required by God and die the sacrificial death necessary to re-create us from the brokenness of sin.

Throughout this passage, Paul compares and contrasts Adam and Christ. By this we are shown that Jesus's righteousness is greater than Adam's sin. This means that what God gives us through Jesus is more assured than what comes through Adam. Grace is more assured than guilt. Life is more assured than death. Justification is more assured than condemnation.

Adam's one act of disobedience brought death, judgment, and condemnation. Jesus's act of obedience brings life, grace, and justification. What Jesus did reverses what Adam did and restores and rebuilds what was ruined. As a believer you are no longer identified with Adam, but with Christ.

The law, however, serves the same purpose whether you are in Adam or in Christ. It shows you where you fall short and points to your need for redemption. But when you are in Christ, your relationship to the law is different—it no longer condemns you. Instead, you receive grace upon grace upon grace. This gift of grace has nothing to do with your actions, but everything to do with what Jesus did for you—making his grace more certain than his judgment.

This gift is the basis for your secure standing. You can know that when you mess up, he will not desert you. He succeeded for you because you will fail. So now when you realize that you lied, you can confess instead of covering it up. When you see how you spoke rudely, you can say you are sorry instead of blame shifting. When you evaluate your heart and know you interrupted someone's story because you wanted the limelight, you can acknowledge this to the Lord. In all your sin, you can go to him. He wants you to see it, to behold him, and to rest assured because of what he did for you.

DAY THREE

Straight to My Heart

Before answering the questions, reread the Scripture, being mindful of insights from the first two days.

:: Based on the Scripture, compare and contrast Adam and Christ.

:: How is Jesus the Second Adam?

:: What is the assurance of your identity being in Christ, not Adam?

DAY FOUR

Back to the Word

Reread the Scripture one more time and then take your time answering the questions below.

:: How does God view you in your sin?

:: How should you relate to him, then, in your sin?

:: How could you help a friend struggling with guilt or shame?

DAY FIVE

Journaling and Prayer

:: Jesus succeeded where you fail, and he did it for you so that his obedience covers your disobedience. What does this mean for you personally? Where has Jesus been perfectly obedient for *you*?

Spend time writing your thoughts.

Prayer

Lord, help me believe that in being united to Christ there is no condemnation over my past, present, or future sin, but instead never-ending grace!

Week 21

What's Your Label?

DAY ONE
Straight from the Word

Read the Scripture and then follow the instructions below.

:: Romans 6:1–14

[1] What shall we say then? Are we to continue in sin that grace may abound? [2] By no means! How can we who died to sin still live in it? [3] Do you not know that all of us who have been baptized into Christ Jesus were baptized into his death? [4] We were buried therefore with him by baptism into death, in order that, just as Christ was raised from the dead by the glory of the Father, we too might walk in newness of life.

[5] For if we have been united with him in a death like his, we shall certainly be united with him in a resurrection like his. [6] We know that our old self was crucified with him in order that the body of sin might be brought to nothing, so that we would no longer be enslaved to sin. [7] For one who has died has been set free from sin. [8] Now if we have died with Christ, we believe that we will also live with him. [9] We know that Christ, being raised from the dead, will never die again; death no longer has dominion over him. [10] For the death he died he died to sin, once for all, but the life he lives he lives to God. [11] So you also must consider yourselves dead to sin and alive to God in Christ Jesus.

[12] Let not sin therefore reign in your mortal body, to make you obey its passions. [13] Do not present your members to sin as instruments for unrighteousness, but present yourselves to God as those who have been brought from death to life, and your members to God as instruments for righteousness. [14] For sin will have no dominion over you, since you are not under law but under grace.

:: Circle the key repetitive words.

:: Which words are being contrasted?

:: For those in Christ, what do you learn about your old self?

:: For those in Christ, what is true about your new self?

DAY TWO
The Word Applied

Have you been labeled a certain way at school? Maybe you are the dumb jock, computer geek, band nerd, snobby rich girl, Miss Perfect, or the teacher's pet. No matter the label, inaccurate or justly given, people define who we are based on our label and we do the same to others. Because of this, labels actually affect the way we live. Just think about how you may either be trying to live up to and maintain the label or striving to drop it and prove that it does not describe you.

The passage speaks to living according to your label. Paul wants believers to see they are no longer labeled with Adam, but are now identified in Christ. A label has been dropped and a new one given. In Adam your label declared you "disobedient one," "slave to sin," "condemned," "judged," and "deserving death." In Christ you are defined by his obedience and the grace of justification, righteousness, and life. You are loved, made whole, and at peace with God.

But don't you still struggle to believe your new label?

Even though we've been talking about how Christ views you, it is hard to reconcile being dead to sin when you know you still sin! What Paul means when he says we have died to sin is that we are no longer slaves to it. Sin is like the cruel master reigning over slaves, the picture seen with Pharaoh in Exodus. But with Jesus's death the chains of sin were broken, freeing you from sin's rule. Its dominating power and authority is now gone and you can fight against its influence.

The "free from sin" and "united to Christ" label means everything that is true about Christ is true of you. It is this label that defines you and should affect the way you live.

If this is the case, why then at times are you still afraid of God? Why do you fear punishment and think God is angry with you or that he will remove his love from you?

If everything that you were in Adam's label has died, then why do you still label yourself according to sins you struggle with? Like, "I'm the one who never measures up" or "I'm the one who lies" or "I'm the one who is obsessive compulsive" or "I'm the one who cuts myself" or "I'm the one addicted to pornography" or "I'm the one struggling with my sexuality."

No! You are the one who is deeply loved by God, declared to be righteous and perfect. You are the one with whom God is well pleased. You are the one who can do nothing now to change any of this because you are labeled HIS.

Start living in the freedom of your new label that Christ won for you. Live for a Father who will only treat you according to his grace.

DAY THREE _____
Straight to My Heart

Before answering the questions, reread the Scripture, being mindful of insights from the first two days.

:: How have you tended to label yourself?

:: How have you seen labels affect you or other people?

:: How should our label in Christ change the way we live?

DAY FOUR
Back to the Word

Reread the Scripture one more time and then take your time answering the questions below.

:: What difference in your life would it make if you found rest knowing that even in your sin your label in Christ doesn't change?

:: How does knowing that grace abounds and that your label does not change even when your sins keep you from wanting to stop sinning?

:: Why do you think understanding this truth does more for "sin prevention" than knowing the law?

DAY FIVE

Journaling and Prayer

:: Considering this week's Scripture, write about what it means for you to have been united to Christ in his death and his resurrection.

Prayer

Lord, thank you for making me yours. Help me live in this freedom and not under the slavery of sin and condemnation anymore.

Week 22

Life Is a Battlefield

DAY ONE

Straight from the Word

Read the Scripture and then follow the instructions below.

:: Romans 6:11–23

[11] So you also must consider yourselves dead to sin and alive to God in Christ Jesus.

[12] Let not sin therefore reign in your mortal body, to make you obey its passions. [13] Do not present your members to sin as instruments for unrighteousness, but present yourselves to God as those who have been brought from death to life, and your members to God as instruments for righteousness. [14] For sin will have no dominion over you, since you are not under law but under grace. [15] What then? Are we to sin because we are not under law but under grace? By no means! [16] Do you not know that if you present yourselves to anyone as obedient slaves, you are slaves of the one whom you obey, either of sin, which leads to death, or of obedience, which leads to righteousness? [17] But thanks be to God, that you who were once slaves of sin have become obedient from the heart to the standard of teaching to which you were committed, [18] and, having been set free from sin, have become slaves of righteousness. [19] I am speaking in human terms, because of your natural limitations. For just as you once presented your members as

slaves to impurity and to lawlessness leading to more lawlessness, so now present your members as slaves to righteousness leading to sanctification. ²⁰ For when you were slaves of sin, you were free in regard to righteousness. ²¹ But what fruit were you getting at that time from the things of which you are now ashamed? For the end of those things is death. ²² But now that you have been set free from sin and have become slaves of God, the fruit you get leads to sanctification and its end, eternal life. ²³ For the wages of sin is death, but the free gift of God is eternal life in Christ Jesus our Lord.

:: Underline at least three commands given to us.

:: What is being contrasted throughout the passage?

:: How is the former condition of those now in Christ described?

:: According to God's work in us, what is the present condition of those in Christ?

DAY TWO

The Word Applied

Audrey is home on a Friday night after not being included in plans with some friends. Feeling depressed, she indulges in a half pint of ice cream and contemplates eating more because of the temporary satisfaction it brought. She rationalizes the binge eating with the thought of either increasing her exercise time the next day or simply just throwing it up. This puts Audrey at a crossroads with sin seeking to capture her.

Jack is surfing the Internet when something catches his eye and arouses a desire. The longer he looks, the stronger his desire grows. He debates clicking on the link that will take him to more. Now Jack is at a crossroads with sin seeking to capture him.

In both cases it takes work and effort to serve sin. Likewise, it takes work and effort to serve God. However, the idea that the Christian life is a battlefield has been lost and the threat and power of sin not taken seriously enough. Instead, we often remain comfortable in our Christian bubble where we pretend life is great and free of struggles with sin. To everyone else it looks like we have it all together.

But that is not true for you or anyone else. So what does it look like to withstand the battle?

Paul says you must first remember your label identifying you as "in Christ." To do so you must engage your mind as a powerful weapon. This is where the conflict starts, and it is there we need to replace sin's lies with God's truth. But if you are not saturating your mind with God's Word, you won't recognize the lies and will be led into sin.

You cannot underestimate the power of sin seeking to rule you. When you fail to fight against it, it will creep in and invade. Once in the door, a little sin always leads to more sin. Think of it this way: By lifting weights you build more muscle mass each time you work out. If you go too many days or weeks without lifting, your muscles start to atrophy. Let sin atrophy. The more often you deny its power and influence in your life, the easier it will be to resist temptation.

Going back to the mental battle—Paul appeals to our intellect to consider the "fruit" that sin produces—guilt, shame, regret, and lack of love, joy, or peace. Sin will suck life from you and wreak havoc on your soul.

Have you experienced the effects? Is it worth it?

True life and freedom are found only with God as your authority. Unlike sin that sets out to destroy, he rules with grace. And because of his kindness and compassion to you, he will never treat you according to what your sin deserves.

DAY THREE

Straight to My Heart

Before answering the questions, reread the Scripture, being mindful of insights from the first two days.

:: How is the Christian life a battlefield?

:: What happens when you do not go to battle against sin?

:: What lies does Satan whisper to you about your sins that need to be replaced by the truth of God's Word?

DAY FOUR

Back to the Word

Reread the Scripture one more time and then take your time answering the questions below.

:: What effect does your sin have on your relationship with God?

:: What effect does your sin have on your relationship with others?

:: What does it mean to be a slave to God and not sin?

DAY FIVE

Journaling and Prayer

:: In the Day 2 devotional reading, rhetorical questions were posed about the bad fruit (guilt, shame, regret, and lack of love, joy, or peace) produced by sin. Today write your answers to these questions: How have you experienced the effects of sin? Is it (sin) worth it?

Prayer

Lord, help me to see sin for what it is, and give me the desire and ability to fight it.

Week 23

Struggling Equals Progress

DAY ONE

Straight from the Word

Read the Scripture and then follow the instructions below.

:: Romans 7:5–25

[5] For while we were living in the flesh, our sinful passions, aroused by the law, were at work in our members to bear fruit for death. [6] But now we are released from the law, having died to that which held us captive, so that we serve in the new way of the Spirit and not in the old way of the written code.

[7] What then shall we say? That the law is sin? By no means! Yet if it had not been for the law, I would not have known sin. For I would not have known what it is to covet if the law had not said, "You shall not covet." [8] But sin, seizing an opportunity through the commandment, produced in me all kinds of covetousness. For apart from the law, sin lies dead. [9] I was once alive apart from the law, but when the commandment came, sin came alive and I died. [10] The very commandment that promised life proved to be death to me. [11] For sin, seizing an opportunity through the commandment, deceived me and through it killed me. [12] So the law is holy, and the commandment is holy and righteous and good.

¹³ Did that which is good, then, bring death to me? By no means! It was sin, producing death in me through what is good, in order that sin might be shown to be sin, and through the commandment might become sinful beyond measure. ¹⁴ For we know that the law is spiritual, but I am of the flesh, sold under sin. ¹⁵ For I do not understand my own actions. For I do not do what I want, but I do the very thing I hate. ¹⁶ Now if I do what I do not want, I agree with the law, that it is good. ¹⁷ So now it is no longer I who do it, but sin that dwells within me. ¹⁸ For I know that nothing good dwells in me, that is, in my flesh. For I have the desire to do what is right, but not the ability to carry it out. ¹⁹ For I do not do the good I want, but the evil I do not want is what I keep on doing. ²⁰ Now if I do what I do not want, it is no longer I who do it, but sin that dwells within me.

²¹ So I find it to be a law that when I want to do right, evil lies close at hand. ²² For I delight in the law of God, in my inner being, ²³ but I see in my members another law waging war against the law of my mind and making me captive to the law of sin that dwells in my members. ²⁴ Wretched man that I am! Who will deliver me from this body of death? ²⁵ Thanks be to God through Jesus Christ our Lord! So then, I myself serve the law of God with my mind, but with my flesh I serve the law of sin.

:: Identify and circle three repetitive key words in the passage.

:: What is the conflict in the passage?

:: Why do we continue to do that which we don't want to do?

:: Write down any thoughts or questions.

DAY TWO
The Word Applied

Route 66 is a well-traveled American highway that stretches across the country from the East Coast to California, cutting right through the city where I live. Just east of town on the highway, a sixty-six-foot architectural sculpture of a soda bottle welcomes visitors to a landmark gas station turned restaurant/soda shop called Pops. People love taking pictures in front of the bottle, though its soaring height makes capturing the whole thing impossible unless you stand way back. Climbing on it would make for a cooler photo op, but a nearby sign reads "Please do not climb on the bottle."

If you see that sign or one stating "Keep Off the Grass," "No Trespassing," or "Adults Only," what do you want to do? Do you have an overwhelming desire to do the exact opposite—to climb the bottle, walk on the grass, or enter where you are not permitted? Why is this?

Passages throughout the Bible and here in Romans state that the law actually arouses sinful desires within us. So when you are told you can't or shouldn't do something, your sinful heart rebels. As we discovered in past weeks, the believer is no longer ruled by sin, yet the inward struggle remains. And at times its power and presence is so strong that even when we want to do the right thing, sin wins out.

This creates a tension within every Christian—a tension that is very real and very normal. In fact, this struggle is the description of the normal Christian life. Remember this life is lived on the battlefield where there will never be constant victory over sin. Since this is the case, it is important to examine what maturing as a Christian really looks like.

Contrary to what many believe, struggling with sin is NOT a sign of backsliding in your Christian walk. It's actually the sign of spiritual progress! The more mindful you are of the internal conflict, the more you realize how powerless you are to defeat sin on your own. This awareness will lead to less self-reliance and more crying out for God's help.

The ongoing struggle proves the Spirit is at work within you. If you were still a "slave to sin," there would be no struggle! The temptation wouldn't be a temptation because you would just do it. For instance, let's say you are taking a chemistry test and look up to see the paper of the smart girl sitting in front of you in plain view. The formula she wrote down is different from what you thought, so you change your answer. There was no struggle or temptation in doing so. But if the Spirit were working in your heart, there would be. It would be a temptation warded off only by God's grace and power within you.

Do you see how conflict, struggle, and temptation wage war inside you? The law reveals and defines sin, showing us how unlike God we really are. Until you see sin for what it really is, you won't hate it. But the more you begin to hate a particular sin, the more motivated you will be to fight it. Again, this does not come from your own resolve; it is only by God's grace, power, and strength that you will be delivered from certain temptations and sins.

So the law and the struggle are good. The more you see inside your heart, the more you see your need for a Savior. This deepening dependence on him is progress and the sign of maturing!

DAY THREE

Straight to My Heart

Before answering the questions, reread the Scripture, being mindful of insights from the first two days.

:: According to this week's passage, what does the law reveal to be true about you?

:: Why is seeing your sin a good thing?

:: What would it look like for you to stop loving a particular sin?

DAY FOUR

Back to the Word

Reread the Scripture one more time and then take your time answering the questions below.

:: If the ongoing struggle with sin—rather than victory—characterizes the normal Christian life, what must God want most from us?

:: Romans 7:18 states that you do not have the ability to carry out what is right. So where must your hope be placed? Where must it not be placed?

:: How does this week's lesson challenge or change your thinking about living the victorious Christian life?

DAY FIVE

Journaling and Prayer

:: Romans 7:15 talks about the struggle of still doing the things we hate. Write about where you have seen this tension in your own life recently.

Prayer

Lord, use the law to show me my need. Help me hate my sin and grow in dependence of you.

Week 24

What Is a "Good" Christian (Not)

DAY ONE

Straight from the Word

Read the Scripture and then follow the instructions below.

Note: Circumcision in the Galatians 5 passage is used metaphorically for seeking justification in the law. In other words, trying to get God's favor by something you do.

:: Galatians 3:1–6

¹ O foolish Galatians! Who has bewitched you? It was before your eyes that Jesus Christ was publicly portrayed as crucified. ² Let me ask you only this: Did you receive the Spirit by works of the law or by hearing with faith? ³ Are you so foolish? Having begun by the Spirit, are you now being perfected by the flesh? ⁴ Did you suffer so many things in vain—if indeed it was in vain? ⁵ Does he who supplies the Spirit to you and works miracles among you do so by works of the law, or by hearing with faith— ⁶ just as Abraham "believed God, and it was counted to him as righteousness"?

:: Galatians 5:1–6

¹ For freedom Christ has set us free; stand firm therefore, and do not submit again to a yoke of slavery. ² Look: I, Paul, say to you that if you accept circumcision [trying to gain God's favor by something you do],

Christ will be of no advantage to you. [3] I testify again to every man who accepts circumcision that he is obligated to keep the whole law. [4] You are severed from Christ, you who would be justified by the law; you have fallen away from grace. [5] For through the Spirit, by faith, we ourselves eagerly wait for the hope of righteousness. [6] For in Christ Jesus neither circumcision nor uncircumcision [what you do or don't do] counts for anything, but only faith working through love.

:: In the Galatians 3 passage, what have the Galatians fallen back into believing?

:: In the Galatians 5 passage, circle what Christ has freed us from.

:: Underline Galatians 5:1, as it serves as the Scripture memory for Part II of this book.

:: Spend a few minutes memorizing it and then write it down below.

DAY TWO
The Word Applied

Everyone considers Johnny to be a really strong Christian. They think he always does what is right, never struggles with doubt, or has a bad day. His perceived goodness makes his friends feel like they can't measure up to his standards. So on Tuesday when they meet for bagels and accountability before school, they often lie about how well they are walking with the Lord, fearing that they will be judged otherwise.

Can you relate? Do you think some people are better Christians than you because they appear to have it all together and you know you don't? Do you feel like you need to work harder to measure up? Maybe it's time to look closer at what we call a "good" Christian.

The "good Christian" label is given to those who behave as we think a Christian should. They typically obey all the rules, are involved in all the Christian groups, witness to others, and are always upbeat and positive. But thinking that this is what is required is the yoke of slavery Paul addresses in our passage. It is moralism, not Christianity.

Moralism is the *appearance of looking good*, doing the right thing, and keeping the rules. It is focusing on external behavior without knowledge or regard for what is really happening in the heart. Just as the Pharisees used circumcision as the indicator of one's right standing with God, our tendency is to look simply at outer behaviors to determine how "on fire" for the Lord one is. This focus leads us to cover up our sin in order to portray ourselves as "good" to others. But it takes a lot of work to appear "perfect," a lot of self-righteous effort, a lot of living the Christian life as if we aren't needy and broken.

We give lip service to declaring that Christ alone saves, but we fail to live out the fact that Christ alone perfectly fulfilled God's law for us. We act as if our standing before God is based on what we do. So instead of talking honestly about our struggles and admitting our sin to one another, we try to live the perfect external life, follow all the rules, attend all the Bible studies, and tweet out Bible verses.

These things are not bad in and of themselves. The problem is that in your effort to live the perfect Christian life through your own obedience and outward performance, you have begun to live as if you don't need Jesus anymore. As if you're really not that broken, needy, or sinful. As if you don't really need Jesus's sacrifice on the cross.

With this focus, being a good witness by your holiness becomes more important than displaying to others your brokenness and need for a Savior. You give the impression to others that you have it all together, even though you know you really don't. So the witness inadvertently points to your "goodness," not his.

Instead of resting in your identity as God's child, you go back to being a slave. A slave is never sure he has done enough to please his master, so he always has to work harder. However, a son rests in his standing by virtue of birth. Come out from under the bondage of trying to work to please God. Jesus alone earned God's favor for you, eliminating the need for striving to earn the badge of "good" Christian.

DAY THREE

Straight to My Heart

Before answering the questions, reread the Scripture, being mindful of insights from the first two days.

:: Why do you feel like you are not a good enough Christian at times?

:: What is moralism and why is it not true Christianity?

:: How does moralism put you in bondage to the "yoke of slavery"?

DAY FOUR   _____
Back to the Word

:: Reread the Scripture passage and then continue memorizing Galatians 5:1. When you think you have it, write it out below.

:: How is a true Christian different from what is typically thought to be evidence of a "good" Christian?

:: Why do you think Christian teaching based on your performance instead of Christ's work for you is destructive to the church?

DAY FIVE

Journaling and Prayer

:: Reflect on what the Lord has been teaching you this week. How have you seen moralistic teaching harm you, other believers, or society in general? Does this teaching seem more prevalent? If so, why do you think that is?

Prayer

Lord, thank you that your love for me is not based on my own effort and good works, but on the perfect work of your Son on my behalf.

Week 25

Fully Free

DAY ONE

Straight from the Word

Read the Scripture and then follow the instructions below.

Note: Though some of this week's passage was read last week, please read again paying special attention to verse 1. As a reminder, circumcision metaphorically refers to trying to get God's favor by something you do; your performance.

:: Galatians 5:1–13

[1] For freedom Christ has set us free; stand firm therefore, and do not submit again to a yoke of slavery. [2] Look: I, Paul, say to you that if you accept circumcision, Christ will be of no advantage to you. [3] I testify again to every man who accepts circumcision that he is obligated to keep the whole law. [4] You are severed from Christ, you who would be justified by the law; you have fallen away from grace. [5] For through the Spirit, by faith, we ourselves eagerly wait for the hope of righteousness. [6] For in Christ Jesus neither circumcision nor uncircumcision counts for anything, but only faith working through love. [7] You were running well. Who hindered you from obeying the truth? [8] This persuasion is not from him who calls you. [9] A little leaven leavens the whole lump. [10] I have confidence in the Lord that you will take no other view, and the one who is troubling you will bear the penalty, whoever he is. [11] But if I, brothers, still preach circumcision, why am I still being

persecuted? In that case the offense of the cross has been removed. [12] I wish those who unsettle you would emasculate themselves! [13] For you were called to freedom, brothers. Only do not use your freedom as an opportunity for the flesh, but through love serve one another.

:: Once again underline Galatians 5:1 and practice your memorization of it.

:: Underline what we have in Christ Jesus that is the only thing that matters.

:: In your own words, what counts as nothing in Christ Jesus?

:: Summarize the main idea.

DAY TWO

The Word Applied

Mason and Hannah started dating at the beginning of their junior year. Though both are Christians, after a few months they began to struggle physically. They knew what they were doing was sinful outside of marriage, but instead of confessing their sin to God and asking for help to stop, they each tried to cover up their guilt by becoming more involved in their youth group. From outward appearances, no one would ever suspect this couple is struggling.

Why do they not turn to God in their sin? Why do they feel like they have to cover up their sin by their outward performance? Why do you do the same thing in your sin?

We talked last week about the yoke of slavery we live under when we base our standing before God on our own performances. But in our sinfulness, it is so easy to fall back under that yoke and fear what God or others will think if they learn what we know about ourselves. When that happens, when we try to cover and hide, we are no longer free. We are no longer living as sons and daughters of the King, but as slaves.

So we must remember again, what did Christ's death set us free from? Fears!

Jesus set you free from facing sin's penalty—free from the fear of facing God's wrath. Along with that comes the freeing truth that your sin will not cause him to abandon you. You are free from the fear that he will love you less, punish you, or reject you. And you are free from the fear that you must perform to make up for any less-than-perfect offense.

Jesus lived the perfect life of obedience not as your example to follow, but as your substitute. He became the object of God's wrath, abandoned on the cross in order to pay the debt of every sin you've ever committed and ever will. He accomplished this completely to set you free.

Just as a young child who has fallen and hurt himself runs screaming to his parent, God desires you to run to him in your sin. He came for the weak and broken and needy, not for those who think they have it all together. What you need most in that painful condition is to be comforted, cleansed, healed, and put back together.

This means Mason and Hannah are free to stop pretending. They can go to the Lord in confession without worry that he will reject them for their sin. It means they should be able to go to others and ask for accountability and prayer without fear that they will be looked down on for their struggle. For you, it means being free to fail and still find forgiveness and freedom in the loving arms of your Father who will embrace you unconditionally forever!

DAY THREE

Straight to My Heart

Before answering the questions, reread the Scripture, being mindful of insights from the first two days.

:: As a review from last week, what has Christ freed you from?

:: How does Christ set you free?

:: What situations lead you to continue living enslaved rather than in freedom?

DAY FOUR   _____

Back to the Word

Reread the Scripture passage and then write out once again by memory Galatians 5:1.

:: What would it look like for you in your sin to experience freedom and not fear?

:: How could you help someone else experience freedom and not fear? What do they need to hear?

DAY FIVE   _____

Journaling and Prayer

:: Do you feel like fear or freedom is more characteristic of your life? Why is this? How does this week's study encourage you or stir you to change?

Spend time writing your thoughts.

Prayer

Lord, thank you for not only freeing me from the eternal conse-quences of sin, but for setting me free now, even in my sin, from hav-ing to earn your love.

Week 26

Walking in the Spirit

DAY ONE

Straight from the Word

Read the Scripture and then follow the instructions below.

:: Galatians 5:16–26

[16] But I say, walk by the Spirit, and you will not gratify the desires of the flesh. [17] For the desires of the flesh are against the Spirit, and the desires of the Spirit are against the flesh, for these are opposed to each other, to keep you from doing the things you want to do. [18] But if you are led by the Spirit, you are not under the law. [19] Now the works of the flesh are evident: sexual immorality, impurity, sensuality, [20] idolatry, sorcery, enmity, strife, jealousy, fits of anger, rivalries, dissensions, divisions, [21] envy, drunkenness, orgies, and things like these. I warn you, as I warned you before, that those who do such things will not inherit the kingdom of God. [22] But the fruit of the Spirit is love, joy, peace, patience, kindness, goodness, faithfulness, [23] gentleness, self-control; against such things there is no law. [24] And those who belong to Christ Jesus have crucified the flesh with its passions and desires. [25] If we live by the Spirit, let us also keep in step with the Spirit. [26] Let us not become conceited, provoking one another, envying one another.

:: Underline all that is true when you walk by the Spirit.

:: Make five observations from the passage about the flesh.

:: Circle the fruits of the Spirit.

:: How is bearing any of these fruits possible?

DAY TWO

The Word Applied

Desi heads back to school after break, excited to catch up with her friends. She sits down at lunch to hear Sophie telling all about the new guy she met. As she goes on and on about him, Desi gets irritated and snaps at her. Sophie didn't do anything wrong. It is Desi's own jealous heart that causes her to be irritated as she feels like everything good happens to others.

Logan has a crush on Savannah and is hoping she asks him to the upcoming Sadie Hawkins dance. When she pulls him aside after class, he tries hard not to show his grin. But instead of inviting him to the dance, she inquires about asking his friend Knox. Feeling rejected, Logan shoots down her idea and speaks poorly about Knox. As soon as he speaks he feels horrible. Knox is his close friend and he didn't do anything wrong; it's Logan's own jealous heart.

Once again there is a battle raging between the flesh and the Spirit—the tension a believer feels when you do things you are ashamed of but can't seem to stop, the desire to be different even if complete victory over sin is impossible. What does it mean and what does it look like to "walk by the Spirit"?

First, let's consider "walk." For most people, the simple, mindless motion of walking takes one from place to place throughout the day. It is routine, typically maintained at a steady pace, and generally given no thought. "Walking by the Spirit" is no different in that it is an ongoing, daily routine, a necessary way of life for the believer. It's not a spectacular victory, an emotional high, or a monumental step. It is daily staying connected to Jesus.[7]

But on this walk we encounter sinful temptations and desires ("lusts of the flesh") that are opposed to the Spirit within us. These sinful desires seek to rule us, and sometimes we get knocked down. When this happens, we have stopped walking by the Spirit and are being controlled by the flesh, which produces "bad fruit" or behavior. On the other hand, when we remain in the Spirit, this too is evident, because of the "good fruit" that we bear.

The "fruit" that comes out of you is directly related to your walk. It is the outpouring of what is going on in your heart—good or bad. When you produce good fruit, it is because you are walking and staying connected to him. It is not of your own doing, but the Spirit within you produces the faith that keeps you with Jesus. There is nothing you can take credit for or boast over even though you still try to live as if your righteousness is based on your good works and effort.

Have you ever tried to compensate for your "bad fruit" or sin by doing something good? Maybe you volunteer to do something helpful or you compliment someone you feel guilty for gossiping about. Without realizing it you rationalize that if your "good" deeds outweigh the bad, then you are okay. But what you are really doing is striving in your own effort to please God and, therefore, you cease depending on him.

The ability to bear good fruit comes from the Spirit alone. Even walking in the Spirit and not veering off course is a work of the Spirit.

By God's grace this happens when you recognize your constant need for him to produce this in you.

DAY THREE _____

Straight to My Heart

Before answering the questions, reread the Scripture, being mindful of insights from the first two days.

:: What does it mean to "walk by the Spirit"?

:: What makes walking by the Spirit hard?

:: In what ways have you looked to your own good works and efforts in an attempt to please God?

DAY FOUR

Back to the Word

Reread the Scripture one more time and then take your time answering the questions below.

:: If he produces the fruit, what is your responsibility?

:: What does the type of fruit you bear reveal about your walk with the Lord?

:: When someone else's bad fruit affects you, what would be a good prayer for them and for you?

DAY FIVE

Journaling and Prayer

:: If "walking by the Spirit" is an ongoing, daily routine necessary for the believer, evaluate how you spend your time each day and then ask God to help you make changes to better abide in him.

Prayer

Lord, I praise you that you never leave me to myself, but you even give me the ability to stay connected to you and walk by your Spirit.

Week 27

Sons and Daughters
of the King

DAY ONE
Straight from the Word
Read the Scripture and then follow the instructions below.

:: Romans 8:12–28

[12] So then, brothers, we are debtors, not to the flesh, to live according to the flesh. [13] For if you live according to the flesh you will die, but if by the Spirit you put to death the deeds of the body, you will live. [14] For all who are led by the Spirit of God are sons of God. [15] For you did not receive the spirit of slavery to fall back into fear, but you have received the Spirit of adoption as sons, by whom we cry, "Abba! Father!" [16] The Spirit himself bears witness with our spirit that we are children of God, [17] and if children, then heirs—heirs of God and fellow heirs with Christ, provided we suffer with him in order that we may also be glorified with him.

[18] For I consider that the sufferings of this present time are not worth comparing with the glory that is to be revealed to us. [19] For the creation waits with eager longing for the revealing of the sons of God. . . . [24] For in this hope we were saved. Now hope that is seen is

not hope. For who hopes for what he sees? [25] But if we hope for what we do not see, we wait for it with patience.

[26] Likewise the Spirit helps us in our weakness. For we do not know what to pray for as we ought, but the Spirit himself intercedes for us with groaning too deep for words. [27] And he who searches hearts knows what is the mind of the Spirit, because the Spirit intercedes for the saints according to the will of God. [28] And we know that for those who love God all things work together for good, for those who are called according to his purpose.

:: Circle the key repetitive words in the passage.

:: Make five observations about the Spirit.

:: What inheritances come with being children of God?

:: Write down your thoughts about these inheritances.

DAY TWO
The Word Applied

Have you ever imagined what it would be like if you had a famous parent? Maybe you do! It sounds pretty cool even to think about some of the perks that accompany fame: getting free passes to all sorts of big events, traveling, meeting other famous people, being photographed by the paparazzi, and then showing up on the "Trending Now" section of Yahoo! Receiving free meals at expensive restaurants or free clothing and products just because of the privilege of your family.

To be a child of the King is no different!

If you are in Christ, you are an heir of God the Father. Everything God has granted his Son, you have also inherited. That includes his identity and his righteousness. And it means when you fail to "walk by the Spirit" and are controlled by fleshly desires, you have his grace and forgiveness.

There will never be a separation between you and God. When you disobey or disappoint a parent, you may feel a distance or separation. But God is not like that. He has already delivered the verdict declaring you justified. That verdict will not change, despite the fact you still mess up and fall into sin. Nothing you did made you his child, and nothing you do will keep you from being his child.

Again, struggling with sin is actually a sign of your sanctification and growing in holiness. God gave you the gift of the Spirit for your sanctification. When the internal battle wages inside you, it is the Spirit that God uses to convict of sin and to bear good fruit. The Spirit is God's righteousness given to you and the security of adoption by the Father. You can know 100 percent without doubt that you are his because the Spirit indwells you. And the Spirit is your guarantee of the glory that awaits you in heaven.

Scripture tells us too that we are not just heirs, but coheirs with Christ! However, with that privilege and the future promise of being glorified with him comes the call to suffering. No one wants to experience trials, pain, or suffering, but as Christians living in a fallen world we will have those experiences in different ways and varying degrees. This life is not where our hope or home lies, and keeping this mind-set will lead to a greater perspective than the here and now.

Heaven awaits us, and one day we will be joined forever to our Father. There will be no more tears, no more trials, and no more sin. This is ultimately what our hearts long for every time we wish things were different, easy, or perfect here on earth. He has given us these great gifts of inheritance so that we can rest confidently in his goodness. We are, and forevermore will be, sons and daughters of the King.

DAY THREE

Straight to My Heart

Before answering the questions, reread the Scripture being mindful of insights from the first two days.

:: As a child of the King, what does this passage say is your inheritance?

:: Why do you often not consider these inheritances as blessings?

:: What does your response to failure or suffering reveal about whether you are believing God's truths or buying into Satan's lies?

DAY FOUR

Back to the Word

Reread the Scripture one more time and then take your time answering the questions below.

:: As a coheir with Christ, what promises in this passage give you hope?

:: If God works all things together for good for those who love him, what does this tell you about his view of "good" versus ours?

:: What issues are going on in your heart or life that you need the Spirit to intercede for you? Ask him to act on your behalf.

DAY FIVE

Journaling and Prayer

:: If you always lived as a son or daughter of the King, how would things be different? What would you not be afraid of? How do you think you would feel?

Spend time writing your thoughts.

Prayer

Lord, I praise you for the gifts of my inheritance as your child. Help me to live with an eternal perspective.

Week 28

Idol Worship

DAY ONE

Straight from the Word

Read the Scripture and then follow the instructions below.

:: Romans 1:18–32

[18] For the wrath of God is revealed from heaven against all ungodliness and unrighteousness of men, who by their unrighteousness suppress the truth. [19] For what can be known about God is plain to them, because God has shown it to them. [20] For his invisible attributes, namely, his eternal power and divine nature, have been clearly perceived, ever since the creation of the world, in the things that have been made. So they are without excuse. [21] For although they knew God, they did not honor him as God or give thanks to him, but they became futile in their thinking, and their foolish hearts were darkened. [22] Claiming to be wise, they became fools, [23] and exchanged the glory of the immortal God for images resembling mortal man and birds and animals and creeping things.

[24] Therefore God gave them up in the lusts of their hearts to impurity, to the dishonoring of their bodies among themselves, [25] because they exchanged the truth about God for a lie and worshiped and served the creature rather than the Creator, who is blessed forever! Amen.

²⁶ For this reason God gave them up to dishonorable passions. For their women exchanged natural relations for those that are contrary to nature; ²⁷ and the men likewise gave up natural relations with women and were consumed with passion for one another, men committing shameless acts with men and receiving in themselves the due penalty for their error.

²⁸ And since they did not see fit to acknowledge God, God gave them up to a debased mind to do what ought not to be done. ²⁹ They were filled with all manner of unrighteousness, evil, covetousness, malice. They are full of envy, murder, strife, deceit, maliciousness. They are gossips, ³⁰ slanderers, haters of God, insolent, haughty, boastful, inventors of evil, disobedient to parents, ³¹ foolish, faithless, heartless, ruthless. ³² Though they know God's righteous decree that those who practice such things deserve to die, they not only do them but give approval to those who practice them.

:: How is God clearly revealed to all men?

:: List five downward spiraling steps occurring in those who do not honor God.

:: Why does God ultimately give them up?

:: Write your thoughts about what it means for God to give them up.

DAY TWO

The Word Applied

Olivia desperately wants to be associated with a certain group at school. In an effort to be viewed as one of them, she has switched cafeteria tables, leaving behind her true friends. But no matter how cute her outfit or what she says or does to try to impress, she is still not considered part of their inner circle. So she goes overboard in flattering them and building herself up, constantly striving to gain their approval and acceptance.

Hunter has the reputation for being all the girls' best guy friend. He likes that they are always texting and coming to him for advice. On the weekends, he typically hangs out with one or more of them. He isn't dating any of them, although any of them would be flattered to date him. Could it be that having the attention from many beautiful girls feeds his ego—so why settle for only one?

These scenarios seem tame in comparison to what Paul describes in our passage, but it's time to hold the mirror up to our own hearts and see which truths are being revealed. Week after week we have discussed God's unending love and acceptance of you. Hopefully, with the security of your inheritance sinking in, you will be willing and able to take a closer peek at what is going on in your heart when "fleshly" or sinful desires still rule you.

When Paul states, "They exchanged the truth about God for a lie and worshiped and served the created thing rather than the Creator," he is talking about worshiping idols or false gods. In this passage men turned away from God and began worshiping statues, thinking they could deliver something God could not. That sounds so obviously foolish, but we need to see how we do the exact same thing.

You do not bow down to golden animal statues, but you still fall prey to idol worship. An idol is anything that rules or controls your heart, anything you turn to apart from God for identity, security, life, or to meet countless other desires. Without even realizing it, you daily replace God on the throne of your heart, just as Olivia and Hunter did.

For Olivia, popularity and the group's inclusion and approval of her had become her false god. She believed the lie that being a part of this group would bring her what she was after. Hunter's idol was being fueled by the benefits of close association with many popular, pretty girls. Though he wouldn't say he was using them, in a sense he was because their attention fed his driving desire to look good and be liked. He was counting on them to fill him in a way that only God ultimately can.

These are just two illustrations. The sky is the limit in how we bow to idols. Unfortunately, idol worship is an issue in all of our lives. As you begin identifying idols in your heart, it will lead you to more specific confessions and a deeper awareness of your need for a Savior. This, in turn, will give you a deeper love for him as you realize how constantly idols replace him in your heart and how patient he is with you.

DAY THREE

Straight to My Heart

Before answering the questions, reread the Scripture being mindful of insights from the first two days.

:: How would you define idol worship?

:: What are some of the idols you struggle with?

:: What do you seek from those idols and fail to see that only God can provide?

DAY FOUR
Back to the Word

Reread the Scripture one more time and then take your time answering the questions below.

:: If you worship idols because you exchange the truth of God for a lie, what are those lies about God that you believe?

:: How has identifying some of your idols stretched your understanding of the depth of sin and your need for Jesus?

:: What does seeing your own idols tell you about everyone else?

DAY FIVE

Journaling and Prayer

:: How has this passage challenged you? Has your understanding of idolatry changed or deepened?

Spend time writing your thoughts.

Prayer

Lord, please show me what I am worshiping in your place, and help me to see the false gods in my life.

Week 29

More Idols

DAY ONE
Straight from the Word
Read the Scripture and then follow the instructions below.

:: Daniel 3:1–29

[1] King Nebuchadnezzar made an image of gold, whose height was sixty cubits and its breadth six cubits. He set it up . . . in the province of Babylon. [2] Then King Nebuchadnezzar sent to gather . . . all the officials of the provinces to come to the dedication. . . . [3] And they stood before the image. . . . [4] And the herald proclaimed aloud, "You are commanded, O peoples, nations, and languages, [5] that when you hear the sound of the horn, pipe, lyre . . . and every kind of music, you are to fall down and worship the golden image. . . . [6] And whoever does not fall down and worship shall immediately be cast into a burning fiery furnace." [7] Therefore, as soon as all the peoples heard the sound . . . [they] fell down and worshiped the golden image. . . .

[8] Therefore at that time certain Chaldeans came forward and maliciously accused the Jews. [9] They declared to King Nebuchadnezzar, [10] ". . . You, O king, have made a decree, that every man . . . shall fall down and worship the golden image. . . . [12] There are certain Jews whom you have appointed over the affairs of the province of Babylon: Shadrach,

Meshach, and Abednego. These men, O king, pay no attention to you; they do not serve your gods or worship the golden image. . . ."

¹³ Then Nebuchadnezzar in furious rage commanded that [they] be brought [to him]. . . . ¹⁴ "Is it true, O Shadrach, Meshach, and Abednego, that you do not serve my gods or worship the golden image that I have set up? ¹⁵ . . . And who is the god who will deliver you out of my hands?" ¹⁶ [They] said to the king, "O Nebuchadnezzar, we have no need to answer you in this matter. . . . ¹⁷ our God whom we serve is able to deliver us from the burning fiery furnace, and he will deliver us out of your hand, O king. ¹⁸ But if not . . . we will not serve your gods or worship the golden image that you have set up."

¹⁹ Then Nebuchadnezzar was filled with fury. . . . ²⁰ And he ordered some of the mighty men of his army to bind Shadrach, Meshach, and Abednego, and to cast them into the burning fiery furnace. . . . ²⁴ Then King Nebuchadnezzar was astonished and rose up in haste. . . . ²⁵ "I see four men unbound, walking in the midst of the fire, and they are not hurt; and the appearance of the fourth is like a son of the gods."

²⁶ Then Nebuchadnezzar came near to the door of the burning fiery furnace; he declared, "Shadrach, Meshach, and Abednego, servants of the Most High God, come out, and come here!" Then [they] came out from the fire. ²⁷ . . . the fire had not had any power over the bodies of those men. The hair of their heads was not singed, their cloaks were not harmed, and no smell of fire had come upon them. ²⁸ Nebuchadnezzar . . . said, "Blessed be the God of Shadrach, Meshach, and Abednego, who has sent his angel and delivered his servants, who trusted in him, and set aside the king's command, and yielded up their bodies rather than serve and worship any god except their own God. ²⁹ Therefore I make a decree: Any people, nation, or language that speaks anything against

the God of Shadrach, Meshach, and Abednego shall be torn limb from limb, and their houses laid in ruins, for there is no other god who is able to rescue in this way."

:: Circle throughout the name of the main character.

:: Underline all of the main character's actions.

:: What do you think is the underlying reason King Nebuchadnezzar was filled with fury when Shadrach, Meshach, and Abednego didn't worship the golden image?

:: What do you think is the main point of this passage?

DAY TWO
The Word Applied

If you have been taught about Shadrach, Meshach, and Abednego and the fiery furnace, you may have been told that if you remain as faithful and obedient as those three God will always rescue you. But is this how God operates? Does he respond based on our performance?

No. God's love is not dependent on you in any way, and the passage does not teach that it is. To understand what the point is we must start by seeing that it isn't even Shadrach, Meshach, and Abednego who are the main characters. This passage is a story about what is going on in the heart of Nebuchadnezzar, a story of how this king (whose name I am shortening to "Neb") tried to secure his deepest desires.

Neb constructed the enormous gold statue for everyone in the entire empire to come worship. But citizens bowing down to this structure is not really what King Neb was after. While these verses do not explicitly tell us this, the chapters in Daniel leading up to this point show his true intentions—that everyone come bow down and praise him.

His desire to be the most powerful and influential man was his god. That is why when Shadrach, Meshach, and Abednego refused to bow down to the golden image, he took it as a personal insult. They did not view him as he wanted everyone to.

We are just like King Neb. The idols that we set up may not be as blatant, but we make false gods out of our desires just the same. Our hearts become demanding when we don't get what we think we need. And we fight against or threaten anyone or anything that interferes with those wants.

Sometimes it's not that the desire is bad, but it becomes bad when you have to have it at all costs. For instance, the desire to be selected for a certain role in the school musical is not bad. But when you belittle or speak rudely to the person you feel might rob you of the coveted spot, it has become a ruling idol. Or perhaps you are known for always having the best one-liners. Being funny is not bad, but when someone else's humor draws the laughs, do you quickly think of something clever to say? Why is this? Is it because you want the spotlight back on you? If so, there is an idol driving your behavior.

Jeremiah 17:9 states, "The heart is deceitful above all things . . . who can understand it?" To help uncover the often hidden idols controlling you, begin asking pointed questions of yourself, like "Why am I so angry?" Ask God for wisdom and understanding to see your heart rightly, to help you see that whatever consumes and controls your thoughts and actions have reached idol status. Then, when you pinpoint an idol, turn to God in confession and repentance, acknowledging your need of a Savior.

God loves to restore his children and does not hold your sin and false gods against you. Nor did he with King Neb, who finally turned his face to God later in the book of Daniel. And do you know what God did? He welcomed him as his child with abounding grace and mercy!

DAY THREE _____

Straight to My Heart

Before answering the questions, reread the Scripture, being mindful of insights from the first two days.

:: How can a good desire be bad?

:: What other questions will help identify ruling heart desires?

:: If turning to false gods or idols is something we all do, why do you try to pretend otherwise?

DAY FOUR

Back to the Word

Grab a Bible or use your phone and take the time to read more about Nebuchadnezzar's story in Daniel 4.

:: What happened to Nebuchadnezzar in Daniel 4?

:: What have you learned or seen differently in studying the passages this week?

DAY FIVE _____

Journaling and Prayer

:: Write about a situation in which you see a specific idol ruling your heart.

Prayer

Lord, help me evaluate my desires and keep them pure. I ask that by the Spirit I can see the truth about what is going on in my heart when I don't get or have what I want.

Week 30

Worrying Won Over

DAY ONE
Straight from the Word
Read the Scripture and then follow the instructions below.

:: Psalm 46

[1] God is our refuge and strength, a very present help in trouble.

[2] Therefore we will not fear though the earth gives way, though the mountains be moved into the heart of the sea,

[3] though its waters roar and foam, though the mountains tremble at its swelling.

[4] There is a river whose streams make glad the city of God, the holy habitation of the Most High.

[5] God is in the midst of her; she shall not be moved; God will help her when morning dawns.

[6] The nations rage, the kingdoms totter; he utters his voice, the earth melts.

[7] The LORD of hosts is with us; the God of Jacob is our fortress.

[8] Come, behold the works of the LORD, how he has brought desolations on the earth.

[9] He makes wars cease to the end of the earth; he breaks the bow and shatters the spear; he burns the chariots with fire.

[10] "Be still, and know that I am God. I will be exalted among the nations, I will be exalted in the earth!"

[11] The LORD of hosts is with us; the God of Jacob is our fortress.

:: Circle God's name used in any form.

:: Underline the words describing who God is.

:: With this psalm's inclusion in the Bible, what is seen to be true about our human nature?

:: What does this tell you about why we should not fear?

DAY TWO
The Word Applied

Erin's alarm clock sounds, and she buries her head under the covers. She dreads this week that has barely started. How in the world is she going to get her homework done plus the research paper that is due when she has practice, a swim meet, and Drivers' Ed? All the while her friends have no extra responsibilities right now, which means she misses out on their fun after-school plans and will miss the Friday night party they are talking about.

There are times we all have stressful, frustrating days or weeks. And even more than the daily grind of life, sometimes we are consumed by real heartache and tragedy. The Bible tells us not to worry, but how is this possible?

In our passage, the word "refuge" is compatible to a storm shelter and "very present" means concrete or solid. For those living in tornado alley, a region of the United States prone to frequent tornados, you are familiar with the safety a tornado shelter offers. With some tornados, these concrete shelters provide the only hope of survival. This is who God is—our shelter, a concrete help even in the worst times imaginable.

Living in this world you will always be surrounded by chaos, sin, stress, and unrest, yet there is safety in his presence. He is the oasis in the midst of the brokenness, suffering, and pain. He is the "holy habitation" of free-flowing grace and mercy where you can be still and unload your burdens.

Resting in this place is hard because you want to control what is beyond your ability. You say that Christ rules your heart and life, but every time a stressful situation, a challenging relationship, or an unforeseen circumstance pops up, you tend to kick God off his throne. Feeling out of control creates anxiety and fear that often sinks you further into worry, stress, and depression. This cycle continues when anything other than God takes center stage. Being ruled by fear, or controlled by our performance, insecurities, and situations (the idolatry we've talked about) will keep us from experiencing his rest and the safety he provides.

On those days when you are ruled by whatever it is—big or small—that is consuming your mind, the only way you can be still and not fear is to know there is a God who speaks peace into chaos. Remember that his Word tells us he is bigger than everything we face. God surrounds the unbearable surrounding us. The Lord of Hosts, the ultimate Warrior, is with us. The God of Jacob, who has been faithful to his people throughout all generations, is our fortress and refuge.

DAY THREE

Straight to My Heart

Before answering the questions, reread the Scripture, being mindful of insights from the first two days.

:: What trials or things in your life cause you to worry?

:: How is stress or worry a form of idolatry?

:: What would it look like to be still?

DAY FOUR

Back to the Word

Be still and meditate on Psalm 46 again.

:: How can Jesus be your "very present help" and "refuge" in your stress and worry?

:: What comfort comes in being still and knowing he will be exalted?

:: How does this passage calm your spirit this week in whatever your circumstances are?

DAY FIVE

Journaling and Prayer

:: Why do you think the imagery of creation is used as it is in the passage? Does it help you imagine God's power as your refuge and strength? How does it help you in being still?

Spend time writing your thoughts.

Prayer

Lord, help me to be still and know that as the God of the universe you have ordered all things and are over all things. Help me to rest knowing you are in control.

Week 31

No Doubt: Jesus Is Life

DAY ONE
Straight from the Word
Read the Scripture and then follow the instructions below.

:: John 20:19–31

[19] On the evening of that day, the first day of the week, the doors being locked where the disciples were for fear of the Jews, Jesus came and stood among them and said to them, "Peace be with you." [20] When he had said this, he showed them his hands and his side. Then the disciples were glad when they saw the Lord. [21] Jesus said to them again, "Peace be with you. As the Father has sent me, even so I am sending you." . . .

[24]Now Thomas, one of the Twelve, called the Twin, was not with them when Jesus came. [25] So the other disciples told him, "We have seen the Lord." But he said to them, "Unless I see in his hands the mark of the nails, and place my finger into the mark of the nails, and place my hand into his side, I will never believe."

[26] Eight days later, his disciples were inside again, and Thomas was with them. Although the doors were locked, Jesus came and stood among them and said, "Peace be with you." [27] Then he said to Thomas, "Put your finger here, and see my hands; and put out your hand, and

place it in my side. Do not disbelieve, but believe." [28] Thomas answered him, "My Lord and my God!" [29] Jesus said to him, "Have you believed because you have seen me? Blessed are those who have not seen and yet have believed."

[30] Now Jesus did many other signs in the presence of the disciples, which are not written in this book; [31] but these are written so that you may believe that Jesus is the Christ, the Son of God, and that by believing you may have life in his name.

:: What did Jesus say to the disciples when he first appeared to them?

:: Explain from this passage what the term "Doubting Thomas" infers.

:: Underline what Jesus said when he reappeared to all of them eight days later.

:: Make a few observations about this second reappearing.

DAY TWO
The Word Applied

Do you struggle with a constant longing for better, for bigger, for more? Do you chase after things to make you happy, even if just temporarily? Do you know these things to be false gods, yet they still keep taking your heart hostage? How do you combat these unruly desires to be content, satisfied, and fulfilled?

The answer in a nutshell: only by finding "life" in Jesus.

The whole book of John is written for the purpose of seeing that "life" is in Jesus alone. We are told he is the giver and sustainer of life. He is the "true light," the "true vine," the "bread of life," and he is "the resurrection and the life." John uses these visual pictures to drill into our heads his main point of finding life by believing in Christ.

John understands the need of our human heart to hear this repeated in as many different ways as possible. Even those who saw Jesus perform the miracles and heard his teaching firsthand failed to believe. And Thomas, even one of Jesus's disciples and in his inner circle of friends, doubted after missing Jesus's surprise visit following his resurrection. Without seeing for himself, he refused to believe it was really Jesus.

So what did Jesus do? In his grace and mercy he reappeared so Thomas could touch and see the piercings in his hands and side. We are just like Thomas. We believe, yet fail to believe at certain times and in certain areas of our lives.

For instance, in the midst of a trial, do you ever feel like God is distant and doesn't care because the situation keeps getting worse?

Do you begin questioning your belief in a God who allows suffering and pain? Guess what is starting to happen? In this instance you do not believe God is on his throne and that he is in control of all things and cares for his children in the midst of their trials. You have let fear control you and Christ is no longer your life.

In another instance, you are depressed because you didn't make the team you tried out for. Many of your friends made it and now hang out together during and after practice without you. To cope with your disappointment and loneliness, you have been eating out of control. It would be embarrassing if anyone knew how much food you consume every night, so you do it all in secret. What has happened? As silly as it sounds, you have found life in food. You have turned to it as your source of comfort instead of looking to the Lord for his comfort, strength, and mercy.

In everyday situations we forget who God is. We think life will be found somewhere else, so we take our eyes off him and turn to idols instead to fill and satisfy us. We believe with our lips, but fail to believe in our hearts. This is why as Christians we must continue to hear the gospel. Jesus's nail-pierced wounds proved to Thomas—and to you—that he loves you. Seeing again and again what Jesus has done for you is where your belief must be rooted. Only then can you know without a doubt that he is Life.

DAY THREE

Straight to My Heart

Before answering the questions, reread the Scripture, being mindful of insights from the first two days.

:: What does it mean that Jesus is your "life"?

:: What situations or areas in your life cause you not to see Jesus as "life"?

:: What are things you turn to for "life" instead of Jesus?

DAY FOUR

Back to the Word

Reread the Scripture one more time and then take your time answering the questions below.

:: What things cause you to be like a Doubting Thomas?

:: Thinking back to a past lesson, what is our most sure and tangible "witness" to Jesus?

:: Why must we constantly hear the good news of Jesus's perfect life and sacrificial death for us?

DAY FIVE

Journaling and Prayer

:: Think more on how believing you have life in his name (John 20:31) brings you "life." Do you *really* believe this, or does "life" seem to be somewhere else? Be honest with yourself. If elsewhere, where and why?

Prayer

Lord, I believe; help me with my unbelief. Center me on the gospel daily to see life is found only in you.

Week 32

Faith Focus

DAY ONE
Straight from the Word

:: Matthew 14:22–33

[22] Immediately he [Jesus] made the disciples get into the boat and go before him to the other side, while he dismissed the crowds. [23] And after he had dismissed the crowds, he went up on the mountain by himself to pray. When evening came, he was there alone, [24] but the boat by this time was a long way from the land, beaten by the waves, for the wind was against them. [25] And in the fourth watch of the night he came to them, walking on the sea. [26] But when the disciples saw him walking on the sea, they were terrified, and said, "It is a ghost!" and they cried out in fear. [27] But immediately Jesus spoke to them, saying, "Take heart; it is I. Do not be afraid." [28] And Peter answered him, "Lord, if it is you, command me to come to you on the water." [29] He said, "Come." So Peter got out of the boat and walked on the water and came to Jesus. [30] But when he saw the wind, he was afraid, and beginning to sink he cried out, "Lord, save me." [31] Jesus immediately reached out his hand and took hold of him, saying to him, "O you of little faith, why did you doubt?" [32] And when they got into the boat, the wind ceased. [33] And those in the boat worshiped him, saying, "Truly you are the Son of God."

:: Make five observations about the disciples.

:: What emotion is controlling Peter and the other disciples?

:: What strikes you about Jesus in this passage?

:: Write down any thoughts or questions.

DAY TWO
The Word Applied

We have seen how our idols and doubts blind us to the truth that life is found only in Jesus. But even with the intellectual knowledge to combat it, we are humans prone to wander and forget. The reality is we are just like Jesus's disciples in the boat, his right-hand men. In fact, we are no different than any of the great men and women of "faith" mentioned in the Bible.

Imagine being asleep in the boat with the disciples. It is the middle of the night, and you wake drenched, waves crashing over the side of the boat. Any minute the boat will surely capsize and you will all die. Adding to your terror, a ghost walking on the water appears out of nowhere.

This ghost says he is Jesus and tells you not to be afraid. So your buddy Peter retorts that if he is Jesus he should prove it by giving him the ability to walk on the water too. And that is exactly what Jesus does. Peter is commanded to get out of the boat and walk. When even standing on water would be impossible, there he goes walking on the unstable surface of water! You would think this would dispel all disbelief, but only seconds later Peter sees the torrential wind and his fear is back in full force.

This is the picture of the very real storm between faith and fear we all battle. One minute we believe; the next we are filled with doubt. One minute you feel beautiful, knowing you are fearfully and wonderfully made, but then a classmate makes a rude comment sending you into insecure self-absorption. One minute you trust that all things work together for good, but then you get a rejection letter from the college your heart was set on. One minute you are satisfied with all that Jesus has provided for you, but then your friend's new shoes fill you with envy.

How quickly our faith falters to fear!

When Peter stepped out of the boat, his eyes were fixed on Jesus. It was when he took his eyes off him and looked at the storm that he sank. It is no different for us. Our faith falters when we shift our sight off our Savior, casting it back on our own performance, circumstances, fears, insecurities, and doubts. The veil falls back down over our face, blocking our clear sight as we focus on these wrong things in place of Christ.

What happens next is key. When Peter, beginning to sink, cried out for the Lord's help, Jesus reached out his hand and rescued him. This was despite Peter's imperfect, wavering faith. This same powerful God—the One who rescued Peter and calmed the storms—is your ever-present help, no matter what storms or doubts are brewing in and around you. Cry out and ask him to keep your eyes fixed on him. Ask him to help you stay focused on who he is, what he has done, is doing, and will do for you. He is the solid Rock you can stand on and the only sure focus for your faith to remain intact.

DAY THREE

Straight to My Heart

Before answering the questions, reread the Scripture, being mindful of insights from the first two days.

:: Write about a situation where your faith quickly crumbled.

:: What do you recognize about yourself when it comes to having faith when things are hard or when you feel anxious?

:: In reading this passage, what do you see to be necessary for maintaining faith?

DAY FOUR _____
Back to the Word

Reread the Scripture one more time and then take your time answering the questions below.

:: We struggle with fear just as the disciples did, but how can knowing Jesus is present with us help dismantle those fears?

:: How does it make you feel to realize he rescues despite your fears and doubts?

:: Why is staying focused on Christ so hard?

DAY FIVE   _____

Journaling and Prayer

:: Great faith only comes in knowing how great your Savior is. As a reminder for when your faith falters, make a list of who Jesus is for you.

Prayer

Lord, thank you for picking me up even when my faith falters. Help me keep my eyes fixed on you and not on myself and my fears and doubts.

Week 33

Heart Change

DAY ONE

Straight from the Word

Read the Scripture and then follow the instructions below.

:: Ephesians 3:7–21

[7] Of this gospel I [Paul] was made a minister according to the gift of God's grace, which was given me by the working of his power. [8] To me, though I am the very least of all the saints, this grace was given, to preach to the Gentiles the unsearchable riches of Christ, [9] and to bring to light for everyone what is the plan of the mystery hidden for ages in God who created all things, [10] so that through the church the manifold wisdom of God might now be made known to the rulers and authorities in the heavenly places. [11] This was according to the eternal purpose that he has realized in Christ Jesus our Lord, [12] in whom we have boldness and access with confidence through our faith in him. [13] So I ask you not to lose heart over what I am suffering for you, which is your glory.

[14] For this reason I bow my knees before the Father, [15] from whom every family in heaven and on earth is named, [16] that according to the riches of his glory he may grant you to be strengthened with power through his Spirit in your inner being, [17] so that Christ may dwell in your hearts through faith—that you, being rooted and grounded in

love, [18] may have strength to comprehend with all the saints what is the breadth and length and height and depth, [19] and to know the love of Christ that surpasses knowledge, that you may be filled with all the fullness of God. [20] Now to him who is able to do far more abundantly than all that we ask or think, according to the power at work within us, [21] to him be glory in the church and in Christ Jesus throughout all generations, forever and ever. Amen.

:: Make five observations about Paul.

:: Do you think Paul experiences personally what he is praying about for other believers?

:: What in the passage led you to answer the previous question as you did?

∷ Why do you think it is possible for Paul to praise God even though he is apparently suffering?

DAY TWO
The Word Applied

Ethan texted you for help with his science project since you are a whiz at physics. You were happy to help and secretly found great pride in the fact others view you as being so smart. When the grades were posted though, he scored higher than you did. The teacher even wrote glowing remarks about how impressed she was with Ethan's project. How unfair that he is getting the credit for the ideas you gave him! But since you've begun asking yourself probing questions to better evaluate your heart, you see the idols ruling you. The same ones keep resurfacing, and hope for change seems unlikely.

Have you ever had feelings like these? This passage is Paul's second prayer to the Ephesians and one of the most important prayers in the entire Bible because of the hope it offers. It is a prayer for your deep, personal life change. The life change goal Paul is after is that you "be filled with all the fullness of God." But how does that happen and what exactly does that mean?

Notice first what Paul is doing in verse 14—he is bowing before God. This should lead us to see the main focus is not the prayer but the One who is being prayed to. It shows us there is One who rules and one who submits. Paul is willingly submitting to the Father because he rules over all things—not just generally but over you specifically!

That means whatever situation, problem, struggle, or idol is going on within and around you is happening in the realm of his rule. He still sits on his throne. For Christians, this provides great confidence and security, knowing that he is in it with you as your Father. Not only that, but there is purpose to what is happening. Nothing is simply random, coincidence, or bad luck. God is ruling and providentially working to accomplish something in you.

That something is change—heart change. God uses people, temptations, and circumstances to reveal what is happening in your heart. This may mean he wants to expose the sin in your heart so you see more deeply your need for grace. He may want to expose your weaknesses so you see your need for his strength. He may use a trial to show you in a deeper way what trusting him looks like. God wants to bring your heart into close contact with the glories of Christ.

Only Jesus and his glories change us. It is not by our determination to do better, our obedience, or our effort to have more faith; it is all him. He is everything that we are not. He lived a perfect life of obedience and credited this righteousness to *you*. We cannot even begin to grasp this kind of love. But when God's great love captures us, and the realities of who he is and what he has done for us penetrate deep in our heart, transformation occurs.

Now when Ethan receives the credit for your ideas, you can be content to let him receive it and by God's grace actually be genuinely happy for his success. Now when your sin leads to doubting God's love, you can rest knowing you are forgiven. Now when you are faced with conflict and trials, you can find comfort in knowing God will never leave you or forsake you. The power of his love at home in your heart takes root and begins filling you "with all the fullness of God."

DAY THREE _____
Straight to My Heart
Before answering the questions, reread the Scripture, being mindful of insights from the first two days.

:: According to our passage, how is life change possible?

:: What are some of the glories of Christ that transform your heart?

:: How can this alter the way you view different circumstances, trials, struggles, or relationships in your life?

DAY FOUR _____
Back to the Word

Reread the Scripture one more time and then take your time answering the questions below.

:: Tell about a situation you've previously experienced to which you might respond differently as Christ's glories fill your heart.

:: How could Christ's glories invading your heart presently change any relational issues or challenging situations?

:: Ask God for the courage and strength to lay aside any pride, shyness, hurt, or hesitation in order to embody Christ's love to someone this week (maybe even someone who has wronged you).

DAY FIVE

Journaling and Prayer

:: Ephesians 3:20: "Now to him who is able to do far more abundantly than all that we ask or think, according to the power at work within us." Do you believe this? Can you grasp how wide and long and high and deep is his love for you? Why or why not?

Prayer

Lord, consume me with the fullness of your great love so that it shapes my heart to reflect more of you to others.

Week 34

Stand on the Gospel

DAY ONE

Straight from the Word

Read the Scripture and then follow the instructions below.

:: Ephesians 6:10–20

[10] Finally, be strong in the Lord and in the strength of his might. [11] Put on the whole armor of God, that you may be able to stand against the schemes of the devil. [12] For we do not wrestle against flesh and blood, but against the rulers, against the authorities, against the cosmic powers over this present darkness, against the spiritual forces of evil in the heavenly places. [13] Therefore take up the whole armor of God, that you may be able to withstand in the evil day, and having done all, to stand firm. [14] Stand therefore, having fastened on the belt of truth, and having put on the breastplate of righteousness, [15] and, as shoes for your feet, having put on the readiness given by the gospel of peace. [16] In all circumstances take up the shield of faith, with which you can extinguish all the flaming darts of the evil one; [17] and take the helmet of salvation, and the sword of the Spirit, which is the word of God, [18] praying at all times in the Spirit, with all prayer and supplication. To that end keep alert with all perseverance, making supplication for all the saints, [19] and also for me, that words may be given to me in opening my mouth boldly to proclaim the mystery of the gospel, [20] for

which I am an ambassador in chains, that I may declare it boldly, as I ought to speak.

:: Underline the commands in the passage.

:: Why are these commands given?

:: Circle the verb best summarizing how you can be strong in the Lord.

:: Write down any thoughts or questions.

DAY TWO
The Word Applied

Do you live daily like life is war? The instructions are clear for us to prepare by putting on the whole armor of God. But, to understand what that entails, let's revisit the concept of life as a battlefield.

Our struggle with sin, idols, trials, and relationships is a lifelong battle. However, Paul says the real war is actually against the schemes of the devil. And since this world is not our true home, we must do battle in enemy territory.

Satan's desire is for you to stop resting in Jesus, to stop walking in the Spirit, and to retreat from the foundation of God's love. To accomplish this, Satan will use all of your sin, circumstances, and relationships to deceive, accuse, and distract you. His goal is to move you away from believing the gospel. He wants you to think you don't need Jesus. He wants you to think that Jesus condemns you. He lies!

He is the master of lies. Lies that say you need to be perfect to be a Christian. Lies that whisper you will never measure up. Lies that murmur you shouldn't struggle with sin. Lies that chant everybody else has their lives together. Lies that sneer you are a "nobody" so you better prove yourself and make your name known. Lies that taunt no one will ever love you; surely Jesus didn't die and save you?

Oh, how Satan loves filling your mind with doubts and fear! He loves nothing more than to see you flounder and your faith crumble. This is just what he is after. Therefore, you must be ready because this battle is personal and unavoidable. You must stand firm, hold your ground, be still, and be strong. The good news is even this is God's doing. He is the one who will make you strong through the gospel. In fact, every piece of the armor necessary for daily battle is connected to the gospel.

Paul starts with the "belt," the truth of the gospel, because of its prominence in connecting all other pieces of the armor, just as the truth serves essential to standing against the schemes of the devil. The next layer of defense stemming straight from the gospel is Christ's righteousness as your "breastplate." It is his work alone that covers you; without it you cannot stand on your own. The truths of the gospel extend to your "shield" producing faith to trust God in all circumstances. Your "helmet" gives the object (Jesus) of your salvation and trust. The Word of God, your "sword," is the only weapon you need because it is truth. And finally "sandals" so you are prepared and ready, not to retreat but to plant your feet solidly into the peace of the gospel so you can stand firm.

You can now stand on Jesus's death, which paid for the debt of all your sins. You can stand on Jesus's perfect, sinless life, covering you in righteousness so God no longer sees your sin. You can stand on Jesus's resurrection because it is the ground already won for all eternity over sin, death, and the devil. Your security and unwavering peace is found only in the gospel. If you are not grounded in the Word of God and (on your knees) in prayer, you will not be able to stand ready for battle. So "be strong in the Lord and in the strength of his might" and STAND!

DAY THREE

Straight to My Heart

Before answering the questions, reread the Scripture, being mindful of insights from the first two days.

:: How is life like a battlefield?

:: How does Satan feed you lies to move you away from the gospel in certain situations?

:: What did you learn about the necessity of putting on the armor of God?

DAY FOUR

Back to the Word

Reread the Scripture one more time and then take your time answering the questions below.

:: What does it mean for you to stand ready for daily battle?

:: When is it most hard for you to stand strong? Why is this?

:: When you fail to stand strong, what do you need to turn back to and believe?

DAY FIVE

Journaling and Prayer

:: Imagine putting on the full armor of God each morning as part of your getting dressed routine. Why is his armor essential to your day's preparation? Does viewing your daily battles as really against Satan increase your need and motivation to be on guard?

Write down your thoughts.

Prayer

Lord, I can only stand by your strength. Help me depend on you for all things and not my own strength.

Week 35

Endurance to the End

DAY ONE
Straight from the Word

:: Hebrews 12:1–11

[1] Therefore, since we are surrounded by so great a cloud of witnesses, let us also lay aside every weight, and sin which clings so closely, and let us run with endurance the race that is set before us, [2] looking to Jesus, the founder and perfecter of our faith, who for the joy that was set before him endured the cross, despising the shame, and is seated at the right hand of the throne of God. [3] Consider him who endured from sinners such hostility against himself, so that you may not grow weary or fainthearted. [4] In your struggle against sin you have not yet resisted to the point of shedding your blood. [5] And have you forgotten the exhortation that addresses you as sons?

> "My son, do not regard lightly the discipline of
> the Lord, nor be weary when reproved by him.
> [6] For the Lord disciplines the one he loves, and
> chastises every son whom he receives."

[7] It is for discipline that you have to endure. God is treating you as sons. For what son is there whom his father does not discipline? [8] If you

are left without discipline, in which all have participated, then you are illegitimate children and not sons. [9] Besides this, we have had earthly fathers who disciplined us and we respected them. Shall we not much more be subject to the Father of spirits and live? [10] For they disciplined us for a short time as it seemed best to them, but he disciplines us for our good, that we may share his holiness. [11] For the moment all discipline seems painful rather than pleasant, but later it yields the peaceful fruit of righteousness to those who have been trained by it.

:: Draw a box around the verb phrase indicating how we can run the race with endurance.

:: Circle everything mentioned describing who Jesus is and what he has done.

:: List three reasons why God disciplines us.

:: Underline Hebrews 12:1b–2 starting with "Let us also lay aside . . ." Spend some time memorizing.

DAY TWO

The Word Applied

Let's go back to the analogy of running a marathon. Again, as a 26.2 mile race that takes hours to complete, a runner must strategically pace himself. If he starts out sprinting, it is highly unlikely that he will make it to the finish line. He will simply exhaust his energy too early in the race, cramp up, or get hurt. Instead, each runner with proper training must find the pace that he can steadily maintain for the long haul. The race will still be grueling, with various factors that can adversely affect his running, but the goal of crossing the finish line motivates him to endure.

I can tell you that crossing the finish line is emotional and one of the most satisfying feelings I have ever experienced. Even after several races I still feel the same way when it's over— absolutely drained but completely elated at the accomplishment. The months of time, sweat, pain, and endurance leading up to race day made it worth it. And though I, like many runners, care about my finishing time, the real joy is not in the time, but in knowing I've completed the race.

Our Christian walk is much like this—a long road, that we can prepare for but one with unknown twists and turns that easily take us off course. We encounter circumstances that were not part of "our" plan. Sometimes we feel like we are barely moving forward and maybe even going backward in our walk. We get hurt and fall down. We cry out in exhaustion, frustration, and pain. Sometimes trials or sin make plodding along seem impossible, and we may question whether living a life of faith, or life at all, is even worth it.

Life is hard. We are weighed down by our sin, idols, circumstances, relationships, and trials and left here on earth to endure. Yet God, who providentially directs our paths, does not leave us alone. In fact, he sent his Son to endure life in this fallen world for us—to endure the rejection, hatred, mockery, and shame that followed him all the way to the cross. But he did it for the joy set before him, the joy of spending eternity in heaven next to his Father with YOU.

Therefore, fix your eyes on him. He is the object of your faith, the perfecter of your faith, and the encourager for your faith. So when you feel down and discouraged, remember Jesus. When you feel hurt or alone, remember Jesus. When you feel scared, remember Jesus. When you have messed up and feel like a failure, remember Jesus. Whatever the emotion or situation, Jesus understands; he has been there and is with you now.

One more thing to remember: all marathon finishers—no matter how fast or slow or how challenged or at relative ease at the finish— experience the same elation in completing the race. Likewise, though

Jesus accomplished glory first and for us, we get to share in the same triumph! One day, we will join him at the throne!

DAY THREE

Straight to My Heart

Before answering the questions, reread the Scripture, being mindful of insights from the first two days.

:: Explain how the Christian walk correlates to a marathon.

:: What are the "weights" that encumber you and seek to take you off course?

:: What specifically do you need to remember when those "weights" surface?

DAY FOUR

Back to the Word

:: What does it mean to fix your eyes on what Jesus did for you as the only means for running with endurance?

:: Spend some more time going back over Hebrews 12:1b–2 for memory.

:: Do you remember the primary memory verse for Part II? Write Galatians 5:1 out below, going back to review it in Week 25 if necessary.

DAY FIVE

Journaling and Prayer

:: We have reached the end of Part II: My Life Mixed into the Story. Reflect on what the Lord has been teaching you during the past months. How have you grown? What are you struggling with?

Spend time writing your thoughts.

Prayer

Lord, when I am frustrated and tired of life's struggles and sin, help me to remember that you endured this earth before me so that I could share in the eternal glory!

PART III

The Story in Me Lived Out with Others

Scripture Memory:

Therefore be imitators of God, as
beloved children. And walk in love, as
Christ loved
us and gave himself up for us, a fragrant
offering and sacrifice to God.
(Ephesians 5:1–2)

Week 36

From the Outside In

DAY ONE
Straight from the Word

Read the Scripture and then follow the instructions below.

Note: The next three weeks will be spent in Ephesians 2. While you should read the entire passage, focus particular attention this week on the underlined verses, 11–13.

:: Ephesians 2:11–22

[11] Therefore remember that at one time you Gentiles in the flesh, called "the uncircumcision" by what is called the circumcision, which is made in the flesh by hands—[12] remember that you were at that time separated from Christ, alienated from the commonwealth of Israel and strangers to the covenants of promise, having no hope and without God in the world. [13] But now in Christ Jesus you who once were far off have been brought near by the blood of Christ. [14] For he himself is our peace, who has made us both one and has broken down in his flesh the dividing wall of hostility [15] by abolishing the law of commandments expressed in ordinances, that he might create in himself one new man in place of the two, so making peace, [16] and might reconcile us both to God in one body through the cross, thereby killing the hostility. [17] And he came and preached peace to you who were far off and peace to those who were near. [18] For through him we both have access in one Spirit to the Father. [19] So then you are no longer strangers

and aliens, but you are fellow citizens with the saints and members of the household of God, [20] built on the foundation of the apostles and prophets, Christ Jesus himself being the cornerstone, [21] in whom the whole structure, being joined together, grows into a holy temple in the Lord. [22] In him you also are being built together into a dwelling place for God by the Spirit.

Follow the instructions below using only verses 11–13.

:: Draw a box around all that was once true for the Gentiles.

:: How did their status change?

:: What is true for those in Christ Jesus?

:: Write down any thoughts or questions.

DAY TWO

The Word Applied

Chloe couldn't have been happier. Having her driver's license gave her new freedom to hang out with friends after school and stay on the go all weekend. But her fun social life came to a screeching halt when her family had to move—mid-year—to a new state. Chloe felt insecure, lonely, and afraid as she attended a new school where she didn't know anyone. She desperately needed a friend, someone who would reach out to her.

Our passage this week is Paul's letter to the Ephesians, which reminds them of their history as the outsider, the stranger, and the rejected. They were part of the Gentile race, not the chosen race to which God had made his covenant promises. They did not have a national hope of a Messiah, nor were they even familiar with God's promises to save.

It was the Jews who were the "circumcised," the ones who had received the sign and seal of God's gracious promise to save. Perhaps this heritage fostered the Jews' feeling of superiority and pride that led to their hatred of the Gentiles. Even close contact with a Gentile made a Jew unclean and in need of temple cleansing. But God's plan to save his people reached beyond Israel to those from all nations. This included the Ephesians, who had heard and believed in Jesus and were now part of the early Christian church.

Why then does Paul recall to the Ephesians their past—their past as outsiders, strangers, lonely, hopeless, unloved, rejected, and different? What benefit was there to remembering this former condition compared to the privileges they now have in Christ?

The benefit of relating to others! When you put yourself in someone else's shoes, it paves the way for compassion. Just think how you feel when you have been through the same or similar situation someone else is experiencing. You know the hurt and pain so you empathize. And this sensitivity and care tends to push out the normal self-focus. The Ephesians are reminded what it was like to be on the outside as a means for relating to others who are rejected, alone, or living in fear or despair.

To some degree we have all been the outsider: not being invited to a party, not getting asked to the dance, not making the team, not being included in a group, not having the same home life as your friends. Even if it is just the insecurity of not knowing anyone at a party, you have felt what it is like to be alone. Some of you know this feeling too well.

Jesus understands this. He was separated from his Father in heaven when he entered this world to take on all the pain and suffering that we experience to the utmost. Then he hung on the cross, rejected not just by those he came to save, but even his Father. God did this though because he loves you. Jesus became the rejected to bring you in from the outside so you would never be alone, deserted, or separated from him.

Chloe, after being uprooted, now feels drawn to others who are new, who have moved or stand all alone. What Christ did for each of us should give us eyes of compassion for others. Look for those around you who are enduring pain, suffering, feeling lonely, being rejected, or sinking in despair so that you can reach out to them in love.

DAY THREE   _____

Straight to My Heart

Before answering the questions, reread the Scripture, being mindful of insights from the first two days.

:: What are the Ephesians reminded of in verse 12 that you must also remember about yourself?

:: What does it feel like when you have been on the "outside"?

:: Why must we remember our former condition as sinners and outsiders to God's promises?

DAY FOUR
Back to the Word

Reread the Scripture one more time and then take your time answering the questions below.

:: How can understanding what Christ experienced and endured on earth affect you in whatever you are going through?

:: What life change, trial, or suffering have you experienced that has led to greater empathy toward others?

:: Do you know someone who might feel like an outsider or be experiencing difficulty? How can you show that person compassion?

DAY FIVE _____

Journaling and Prayer

:: Do you really see how you were once far off and have been brought to the inside only by his grace? How does this affect you? Why is it good to remember?

Spend time writing your thoughts.

Prayer

Lord, how incomprehensible is your love for me that you rejected your own Son. Because of this, help me show unconditional love and compassion to others.

Week 37

Barriers Removed

DAY ONE

Straight from the Word

Read the Scripture and then follow the instructions below.

Note: Continuing in Ephesians 2 read the entire passage, but this week focus your attention on verses 14–18.

:: Ephesians 2:11–22

[11] Therefore remember that at one time you Gentiles in the flesh, called "the uncircumcision" by what is called the circumcision, which is made in the flesh by hands—[12] remember that you were at that time separated from Christ, alienated from the commonwealth of Israel and strangers to the covenants of promise, having no hope and without God in the world. [13] But now in Christ Jesus you who once were far off have been brought near by the blood of Christ. [14] For he himself is our peace, who has made us both one and has broken down in his flesh the dividing wall of hostility [15] by abolishing the law of commandments expressed in ordinances, that he might create in himself one new man in place of the two, so making peace, [16] and might reconcile us both to God in one body through the cross, thereby killing the hostility. [17] And he came and preached peace to you who were far off and peace to those who were near. [18] For through him we both have access in one Spirit to the Father. [19] So then you are no longer strangers and aliens, but you are fellow citizens with the saints and members of

the household of God, [20] built on the foundation of the apostles and prophets, Christ Jesus himself being the cornerstone, [21] in whom the whole structure, being joined together, grows into a holy temple in the Lord. [22] In him you also are being built together into a dwelling place for God by the Spirit.

Follow the instructions below using only verses 14–18.

:: Draw a box around all that you learn about who Jesus is and what he did.

:: Circle the key word repeatedly used in this section.

:: What is the author's main emphasis in this section?

:: Why do you think the author is stressing what he is to the Gentiles?

DAY TWO

The Word Applied

For the past couple of months David has held a grudge against Sam and stopped hanging out with him. Poor Sam has no idea what he did. Then, through a conversation with someone else, David realized what he believed about Sam wasn't true and he had unfairly dismissed him.

Have you ever falsely accused or gossiped about someone? Have you later gotten to know that person and felt bad about your prejudgment?

It is pride that keeps us from loving others—especially those not like us. We think we are better, often viewing those of different backgrounds, race, socio-economic status, personalities, or interests as beneath us. For example, how do you view someone who attends a different school? Have you stereotyped them to be snobby, rude, losers, or enemies?

The Ephesians were once viewed as enemies to the Jews, but now they are united together in Christ. Jesus experienced God's warfare for us, first and foremost, to remove the barriers between God and man and to give us peace. We all have equal standing in our shared former condition apart from Christ. None of us are better, more deserving, more special, or more loved. None of us can earn grace, which automatically eliminates pride or right standing based on our own perceived goodness. We are all sinners saved by grace. And, we ALL need a Savior.

At the cross the barriers between Christians are removed and we are united together. We are bonded with a common goal. We are all part of the same family, the body of Christ, and called to peace with one another.

What does this mean for you?

Perhaps it means getting to know the kid at youth group who sits alone. Or initiating a conversation with the girl in class whom you've never spoken to because you think she doesn't like you. Or including someone outside your immediate friend circle in your weekend plans. It means not gossiping or judging someone because they act or dress differently. It means reaching out to help someone even if it infringes on what you want to do. It means bragging on someone else and not hogging the spotlight.

Because of his death, the barriers have been destroyed and the implications are limitless. We are no longer separated or isolated from one another. Each of us has been made new in Christ, creating a way for peace and unity between us.

DAY THREE

Straight to My Heart

Before answering the questions, reread the Scripture, being mindful of insights from the first two days.

:: What is the basis for being united in Christ?

:: What is the only way that we will find peace with one another?

:: What specific barriers keep you from loving other Christians who are different from you?

DAY FOUR

Back to the Word

Reread the Scripture one more time and then take your time answering the questions below.

:: How can you better seek to live united to other believers?

:: Considering what is going on in the lives of those around you this week, how can you reach out to love or serve a friend?

:: How can you extend the peace of Christ to a stranger or someone different than you?

DAY FIVE

Journaling and Prayer

:: If the message of Christ is peace, why do you think there is so much discord and hostility even among believers? How can the peace of Christ be recovered?

Spend time writing your thoughts.

Prayer

Lord, please help me see other believers as family members and team-mates that I am united to and called to love.

Week 38

The Church Is Our Family

DAY ONE
Straight from the Word

Read the Scripture and then follow the instructions below.

Note: This final week in Ephesians 2 will be concentrated on verses 19–22. Again, read the entire passage before zeroing in on the underlined verses.

:: Ephesians 2:11–22

[11] Therefore remember that at one time you Gentiles in the flesh, called "the uncircumcision" by what is called the circumcision, which is made in the flesh by hands—[12] remember that you were at that time separated from Christ, alienated from the commonwealth of Israel and strangers to the covenants of promise, having no hope and without God in the world. [13] But now in Christ Jesus you who once were far off have been brought near by the blood of Christ. [14] For he himself is our peace, who has made us both one and has broken down in his flesh the dividing wall of hostility [15] by abolishing the law of commandments expressed in ordinances, that he might create in himself one new man in place of the two, so making peace, [16] and might reconcile us both to God in one body through the cross, thereby killing the hostility. [17] And he came and preached peace to you who were far off and

peace to those who were near. [18] For through him we both have access in one Spirit to the Father. [19] So then you are no longer strangers and aliens, but you are fellow citizens with the saints and members of the household of God, [20] built on the foundation of the apostles and prophets, Christ Jesus himself being the cornerstone, [21] in whom the whole structure, being joined together, grows into a holy temple in the Lord. [22] In him you also are being built together into a dwelling place for God by the Spirit.

Follow the instructions below using only verses 19–22.

:: Draw a box around everything that is true of the Gentiles who are now in Christ.

:: What "structure" is Christ the cornerstone of?

:: Who is being joined together to comprise this "structure"?

:: Circle the prepositional phrase indicating how growing with one another occurs.

DAY TWO
The Word Applied

Do you know the feeling of being away from home for a period of time but ready to be back? Maybe it was for a couple weeks or even just a few days, but isn't it nice to sleep in your own bed again? Nice to see your pets, your friends, eat your favorite foods, do your normal activities—all those things that make home, home to you? And if coming home doesn't have all those comforts, don't we all long for a place where we can rest and feel safe?

Did you know that for a Christian, gathering with God's people in a particular place is "home"? Church is where we worship and hear the preached Word of God and also where we connect with other believers. Whether you realize it or not, we cannot grow without the church. It is more than important; it is absolutely necessary.

Does that surprise you? Not that church is important, but that it is essential to your growth? Yes, all Christians need their home, the church. But the cultural value placed on independence has affected how we relate to God. We tend to think he is great, as long as he fits in our schedule. If it's inconvenient to go to church because of other activities, we think it is no big deal. We can always just watch a service online later or have an extra quiet time.

Remember, we've been re-created as one united body. Though individually diverse, our love of Christ connects us in a deeper way than other relationships. In fact, Paul says we are a family, members of God's household.

Think about how a family home should operate. It should be a safe place where all individuals feel accepted, loved, and respected. It should be a place of grace where we experience forgiveness, not rejection, when we sin. It should be a place where we seek to listen, understand, and help one another. It should be a place where we can let our guard down and cry or have fun with one another.

These characteristics and responsibilities are to be present in the church family too. We must share in each other's joys, pains, and sorrows. When a member is going through a trial, we enter it with them. When we see an ugly side to someone, we learn to deal with each other's faults and accept the bad with the good. When we sin, we must confess and forgive.

In addition to being a family, we are being built into God's holy temple with Christ as the foundation. He is the only solid foundation, the support and strength necessary to grow in grace in a fallen world. Living our messy lives out with each other is hard, and we often fail. But Jesus at the cross stands in the center as our hope.

This truth that Paul tells the Ephesians—and us—about the church is crucial. At some point in the future you will likely leave your family for college, a job, or marriage. You need the church. You need a place that will be home. You need to be a part of the Christian family. Don't wait though to leave home. If you do not attend church, find a "home." If you go to church but have missed seeing its vital necessity, go invest in your "home." We need each other of all ages and stages in the church. God has given us the gift of others to help us see more of him, and he uses us to show more of him to others.

DAY THREE _____

Straight to My Heart

Before answering the questions, reread the Scripture, being mindful of insights from the first two days.

:: What does it mean for Christ to be the cornerstone of the church?

:: Why is gathering with God's people in a local church essential to your growth?

:: How does this challenge you to view church differently?

DAY FOUR _____

Back to the Word

Reread the Scripture one more time and then take your time answering the questions below.

:: In what ways have you seen a church family function like a true family?

:: In what ways do you feel like the church has failed to function like a true family should?

:: What can you do as a teen to invest in the life and body of your church?

DAY FIVE _____

Journaling and Prayer

:: After three weeks spent in this passage, reflect on what the Lord has taught you. If someone asked you what Ephesians 2 is about, how would you answer?

Prayer

Lord, thank you that you are our solid foundation. Help me view my relationships with those in the church of all ages, stages, and person-alities as a family built on you.

Week 39

Mission: God's Glory

DAY ONE
Straight from the Word

Read the Scripture and then follow the instructions below.

:: John 17:6–26

⁶ "I [Jesus] have manifested your name [God's] to the people whom you gave me out of the world. Yours they were, and you gave them to me, and they have kept your word. ⁷ Now they know that everything that you have given me is from you. ⁸ For I have given them the words that you gave me, and they have received them and have come to know in truth that I came from you; and they have believed that you sent me. ⁹ I am praying for them. I am not praying for the world but for those whom you have given me, for they are yours. ¹⁰ All mine are yours, and yours are mine, and I am glorified in them. ¹¹ And I am no longer in the world, but they are in the world, and I am coming to you. Holy Father, keep them in your name, which you have given me, that they may be one, even as we are one. ¹² While I was with them, I kept them in your name. . . . I have guarded them, and not one of them has been lost except the son of destruction, that the Scripture might be fulfilled. ¹³ But now I am coming to you, and these things I speak in the world, that they may have my joy fulfilled in themselves. ¹⁴ I have given them your word, and the world has hated them because they are

not of the world, just as I am not of the world. ¹⁵ I do not ask that you take them out of the world, but that you keep them from the evil one. ¹⁶ They are not of the world, just as I am not of the world. ¹⁷ Sanctify them in the truth; your word is truth. ¹⁸ As you sent me into the world, so I have sent them into the world. ¹⁹ And for their sake I consecrate myself, that they also may be sanctified in truth.

²⁰ I do not ask for these only, but also for those who will believe in me through their word, ²¹ that they may all be one, just as you, Father, are in me, and I in you, that they also may be in us, so that the world may believe that you have sent me. ²² The glory that you have given me I have given to them, that they may be one even as we are one, ²³ I in them and you in me, that they may become perfectly one, so that the world may know that you sent me and loved them even as you loved me. ²⁴ Father, I desire that they also, whom you have given me, may be with me where I am, to see my glory that you have given me because you loved me before the foundation of the world. ²⁵ O righteous Father, even though the world does not know you, I know you, and these know that you have sent me. ²⁶ I made known to them your name, and I will continue to make it known, that the love with which you have loved me may be in them, and I in them."

:: Underline what Jesus has done that he is recalling to the Father.

:: Circle the things Jesus is asking the Father to do for his children.

:: What common theme or phrases run throughout the passage?

:: Write down any thoughts or questions.

DAY TWO
The Word Applied

We are listening in again on Jesus's high priestly prayer to the Father prior to his arrest and crucifixion. Through his words, we learn that we have always been on God's mind; and from all eternity past, the plan was to send Jesus to live and die for us. Now in just a few short hours Jesus will be betrayed, beaten, and broken. Even still, his concern is not for himself, but for his people whom he will leave here on earth.

Jesus knows that we will sin, experience the consequences of sin, and suffer the pain and trials of life in a fallen world. Yet it is not without purpose that we are left to endure all that comes our way. Jesus is asking God to set apart and sanctify his people for the specific mission of proclaiming and displaying him to a hostile world. To set apart his people to glorify his name, just as he glorified the Father.

If you are set apart for a mission, what does that mean for you—a teenager, wherever you live?

Being set apart does not mean being separated from the world; it is actually the opposite. You are to be in the world so the world can see Jesus through you. That means you cannot stay in your own little holy huddles to keep from being contaminated by worldliness and the world's sin, though you must be careful not to be conformed by it or partake in the sinful behavior. You have been set apart for holiness.

Growing in holiness, or grace, hinges more on loving others than living isolated, moral lives. It actually requires you to get involved in the lives (and the mess) of those around you, those God has put in your path.

The world often looks at Christians and doesn't see anything different about the way we live our lives, which in turn causes others to think little or nothing of God. But think for a moment what happens if you reach out to someone who needs a friend. Let's say your neighbor's parents are in the midst of an ugly divorce. Most people don't get involved because they either don't know what to say or do, or they just think it's better to mind their own business. What an opportunity, though, to show the love of Christ to those who are hurting, and to offer the hope they desperately need and will only find in Jesus.

Everyday in big and small ways you have these opportunities. When you view your life with the mission of glorifying God, you will reflect Jesus to others. You will be different and the world will take notice. You will be less self-focused and tempted by false gods. You will grow in holiness and grace. You will be set apart.

This happens not as a result of learning to love others better, but as a result of staying in the Word so that you are reminded again and again how deeply he loves *you*. Understanding his love is what changes you and will produce in you a deeper love for others. The more you are captivated by God's glory, the more he will use you for the good of others.

DAY THREE

Straight to My Heart

Before answering the questions, reread the Scripture, being mindful of insights from the first two days.

:: What does it mean to be set apart for holiness?

:: Why does Jesus ask God that we be sanctified (or set apart) in the truth?

:: According to John 17:17–23, how do we grow in holiness and loving others?

DAY FOUR

Back to the Word

Reread the Scripture one more time and then take your time answering the questions below.

:: How does understanding your earthly mission give deeper meaning to your time, experiences, and relationships?

:: In what specific ways can you reflect God's glory to someone around you?

(For example, could you reach out to someone you notice is upset in one of your classes? Could you take your little brother for a surprise ice cream run or send a handwritten note of encouragement to someone?)

:: Ask God for the opportunity to put some of these ideas into action!

DAY FIVE   _____

Journaling and Prayer

:: May you be captivated by God's glory and grace and great love for you! In thinking about this, list all that comes to mind about who he is. You may even dog-ear this page as a reference when you need to be reminded.

Prayer

Lord, you have given me a mission by setting me apart for your glory. Remind me daily of your great love for me so that I may, in turn, show your love to others.

Week 40

Christ's Ambassador

DAY ONE

Straight from the Word

Read the Scripture and then follow the instructions below.

:: 2 Corinthians 5:6–21

[6] So we are always of good courage. We know that while we are at home in the body we are away from the Lord, [7] for we walk by faith, not by sight. [8] Yes, we are of good courage, and we would rather be away from the body and at home with the Lord. [9] So whether we are at home or away, we make it our aim to please him. [10] For we must all appear before the judgment seat of Christ, so that each one may receive what is due for what he has done in the body, whether good or evil.

[11] Therefore, knowing the fear of the Lord, we persuade others. But what we are is known to God, and I hope it is known also to your conscience. [12] We are not commending ourselves to you again but giving you cause to boast about us, so that you may be able to answer those who boast about outward appearance and not about what is in the heart. [13] For if we are beside ourselves, it is for God; if we are in our right mind, it is for you. [14] For the love of Christ controls us, because we have concluded this: that one has died for all, therefore all have

died; [15] and he died for all, that those who live might no longer live for themselves but for him who for their sake died and was raised.

[16] From now on, therefore, we regard no one according to the flesh. Even though we once regarded Christ according to the flesh, we regard him thus no longer. [17] Therefore, if anyone is in Christ, he is a new creation. The old has passed away; behold, the new has come. [18] All this is from God, who through Christ reconciled us to himself and gave us the ministry of reconciliation; [19] that is, in Christ God was reconciling the world to himself, not counting their trespasses against them, and entrusting to us the message of reconciliation. [20] Therefore, we are ambassadors for Christ, God making his appeal through us. We implore you on behalf of Christ, be reconciled to God. [21] For our sake he made him to be sin who knew no sin, so that in him we might become the righteousness of God.

:: Underline what was accomplished for us through the death of Christ.

:: Why was Christ made to be sin?

:: Circle what else is true for those who are in Christ.

:: What central idea is being conveyed through this passage?

DAY TWO

The Word Applied

In the United States, the president appoints ambassadors as official representatives of the US to each foreign country that is part of the United Nations. To serve in this capacity requires the ambassador to live in the assigned country with the task of promoting the policy and goodwill of America. It is the ambassador's top priority to attend all meetings and events in that country to represent and communicate the interests of the US. And depending on the foreign locale, this may not be as cushy as it sounds because many places are unfriendly, hostile, and even war zones.

In much the same way, Christians are called to be ambassadors for Christ. We are to be about him, promoting and extending his glory to all—the mission and opportunities we talked about last week. But there is a problem. What happens when the ambassador isn't in the mood to carry out his job and wants to do his own thing? How nice it would be if he could just take the American flag pin off his jacket lapel, put on a ball cap and T-shirt, and go incognito for a day to take care of his own personal agenda.

Do you ever feel that way—that you don't always want to be Christ's ambassador?

If you do, you are not alone. If we are honest, on most days most of us would rather just live for ourselves. After all, life is hard enough without having to get in the middle of other people's drama. It is a burden when you feel like you have to be mindful of whether others see Christ in you or you appear to be a hypocrite.

It's true, living as Christ's ambassador is not easy or something we can do on our own.

The only right motivation for living as an ambassador comes when the love of Christ is what controls, compels, governs, and constrains us. It was radical for Jesus to give up all of his glory so you could be reconciled to God. Only when this gospel story of the unconditional love of Christ captivates you, do your desires change and compel you to live for his glory and the good of others. It will also constrain you in the sense that it limits you to only wanting to be his ambassador. Your greatest joy will actually be in loving and serving others instead of loving and serving yourself.

For example, you told a woman from church that you would babysit a few children at the foster care agency while their parents attend class. But at the time you agreed to help, you had forgotten about the school event all your friends are going to. With any number of excuses, it would be easy to back out of volunteering. Instead of breaking your commitment though, you resolve that this is an opportunity to love kids who need to feel loved.

Similarly, you are looking forward to sleeping in Saturday before your Eagle Scout project. But then your grandmother calls and asks you to come over early to do some yard work for her. You are disappointed but know your grandmother can't do it alone.

Your response to these situations could've been completely different. However, when the love of Christ controls you, your loyalties change. You want to glorify God by loving and serving others. You fulfill your calling as an ambassador of Christ, not out of duty but love!

DAY THREE _____

Straight to My Heart

Before answering the questions, reread the Scripture, being mindful of insights from the first two days.

:: What does it mean to be an ambassador of Christ?

:: What typically rules your heart when you would rather not be an ambassador?

:: In knowing you don't always feel like serving as an ambassador (nor acting like one), what does this tell you about yourself and your need?

DAY FOUR

Back to the Word

Reread the Scripture one more time and then take your time answering the questions below.

:: According to 2 Corinthians 5:14 how does Christ's love for us control, compel, and constrain us?

:: Tell about a situation or two where you might have responded differently had Christ's love been compelling you as an ambassador.

:: How would your school or community be different if all believers lived as ambassadors?

DAY FIVE _____
Journaling and Prayer

:: Meditate on 2 Corinthians 5:18–19: "Christ reconciled us to himself and gave us the ministry of reconciliation; that is, in Christ God was reconciling the world to himself, not counting their trespasses against them, and entrusting to us the message of reconciliation." What does this mean for you personally? How can you offer the message of reconciliation to someone—specifically or in general?

Prayer

Lord, captivate me by your work on my behalf in both your life and your death so that I am compelled by love to be your ambassador.

Week 41

The Internal Raging War

DAY ONE

Straight from the Word

Read the Scriptures and then follow the instructions below.

:: James 3:13–18

[13] Who is wise and understanding among you? By his good conduct let him show his works in the meekness of wisdom. [14] But if you have bitter jealousy and selfish ambition in your hearts, do not boast and be false to the truth. [15] This is not the wisdom that comes down from above, but is earthly, unspiritual, demonic. [16] For where jealousy and selfish ambition exist, there will be disorder and every vile practice. [17] But the wisdom from above is first pure, then peaceable, gentle, open to reason, full of mercy and good fruits, impartial and sincere. [18] And a harvest of righteousness is sown in peace by those who make peace.

:: James 4:1–6

[1] What causes quarrels and what causes fights among you? Is it not this, that your passions are at war within you? [2] You desire and do not have, so you murder. You covet and cannot obtain, so you fight and quarrel. You do not have, because you do not ask. [3] You ask and do not receive, because you ask wrongly, to spend it on your passions. [4] You

adulterous people! Do you not know that friendship with the world is enmity with God? Therefore whoever wishes to be a friend of the world makes himself an enemy of God. [5] Or do you suppose it is to no purpose that the Scripture says, "He yearns jealously over the spirit that he has made to dwell in us"? [6] But he gives more grace. Therefore it says, "God opposes the proud, but gives grace to the humble."

:: Circle everything in James 4 contributing to quarrels and fights.

:: What phrase in James 3 could all the words you circled in James 4 fall under?

:: How do you see this as friendship with the world and opposed to God?

:: Write down any thoughts or questions.

DAY TWO
The Word Applied

After shopping all day you finally find the perfect dress for the home-coming dance. The color and style are just what you had described to your friends that you wanted. When you text a picture of it to a few of them, Lily comments back that Emma bought the same dress. You think, *WHAT! How could she do that to me? She knew what I was on the hunt for, and she stole my idea. No way am I wearing the same dress, but she should return hers!*

Since elementary school you have played year-round baseball racking up countless hours at the batting cages and tournaments. Finally it's time to try out for the high school team. You feel pretty confident, having heard from older players that your name is being mentioned to fill the vacated shortstop position. But, when the roster is posted, Max is listed in that position with you as backup. *Are you kidding? Max has always played outfield, and now he has stolen my position!*

What is it in each case that leads to the anger? Is it because something was stolen from you, or is something deeper raging inside you?

You can probably figure out the right answer, but you may not understand why yet! The truth is, the problem is not primarily between you and the other person; the real problem is the war going on inside you between your kingdom and God's.

Underneath every relational war is something deeper, a root cause, leading to the sinful thoughts or behavior. In these two situations, anger was aroused when someone interfered with what you wanted. Outraged, you blame it on the other person. The other person is not the problem though; the problem is in your heart. You want what you want, and the fact that you got angry shows your heart being ruled by an unmet desire.

To determine if your desires have become idols, think of it in what author Paul Tripp describes as an open hand or clinched fist.[8] If you are holding so tightly to your desire that you can't let it go, it is ruling you, and its dominating power is what leads to conflict with others.

When you begin to recognize that it is not the people and situations bringing out the worst in you, but your own sinful heart, you will begin living more redemptively with one another. Redemptive living is a pattern of seeking forgiveness and extending grace.

Understanding your own heart gives you a greater compassion toward others, knowing they too have sinful hearts. Then by God's grace when you blow up at someone and realize the war going on internally, you can confess and repent. And by God's grace, when someone reacts out of sin toward you, you will be able to extend the same grace God gives you.

DAY THREE
Straight to My Heart

Before answering the questions, reread the Scripture, being mindful of insights from the first two days.

:: What causes quarrels and fights among you?

:: Considering James 3:14–17, how can you detect the root sin beneath your thoughts and actions?

:: In the given two situations, what might have been the responses had you been living for God's kingdom and not your own?

DAY FOUR

Back to the Word

Reread the Scripture one more time and then take your time answering the questions below.

:: Explain how viewing your desires as being held in a clenched fist or open palm can help you see if you are being ruled by them.

:: In thinking about relational conflicts you have experienced, what desires can you identify as having been held in a clenched fist?

:: When you recognize a ruling desire, what is the solution to loosening its hold on you?

DAY FIVE _____

Journaling and Prayer

:: James 4:6 states God opposes the proud and shows favor to the humble. How does this relate to the conflicts addressed in this passage? Think further about your own conflicts. Where do you see your pride? Write about this and ask God for a spirit of humility.

Prayer

Lord, thank you for continually pouring out your grace on me. Help me hold my desires in an open hand, living for your kingdom and not mine.

Week 42

Fear Factor Freedom

DAY ONE
Straight from the Word

Read the Scripture and then follow the instructions below.

:: 1 John 4:7–21

[7] Beloved, let us love one another, for love is from God, and whoever loves has been born of God and knows God. [8] Anyone who does not love does not know God, because God is love. [9] In this the love of God was made manifest among us, that God sent his only Son into the world, so that we might live through him. [10] In this is love, not that we have loved God but that he loved us and sent his Son to be the propitiation for our sins. [11] Beloved, if God so loved us, we also ought to love one another. [12] No one has ever seen God; if we love one another, God abides in us and his love is perfected in us.

[13] By this we know that we abide in him and he in us, because he has given us of his Spirit. [14] And we have seen and testify that the Father has sent his Son to be the Savior of the world. [15] Whoever confesses that Jesus is the Son of God, God abides in him, and he in God. [16] So we have come to know and to believe the love that God has for us. God is love, and whoever abides in love abides in God, and God abides in him. [17] By this is love perfected with us, so that we may have confidence for the Day of Judgment, because as he is so also are we

in this world. [18] There is no fear in love, but perfect love casts out fear. For fear has to do with punishment, and whoever fears has not been perfected in love. [19] We love because he first loved us. [20] If anyone says, "I love God," and hates his brother, he is a liar; for he who does not love his brother whom he has seen cannot love God whom he has not seen. [21] And this commandment we have from him: whoever loves God must also love his brother.

∷ Make five observations specifically about love.

∷ How is love perfected in us?

∷ From this passage, what appears to be the opposite of love?

∷ Write down any thoughts or questions.

DAY TWO
The Word Applied

How do you handle the feeling that someone doesn't like you? What about your feelings after you've had a conflict or a difference of opinion with someone? For a lot of us we act like a turtle popping his head into his shell for protection. In an effort of self-protection or to save ourselves from being hurt or embarrassed, we withdraw. For the same reasons, we build a protective wall around us and don't let anyone near enough in the first place. We believe they would reject us if they knew what was really going on. So in an effort to remain guarded, we keep them at a distance and reject them first. We are being ruled by fear.

Insecurity is also a by-product of fear. The fear of looking bad or not being accepted may be why you stay quiet. If you fly under the radar and remain anonymous, maybe no one will notice you. Or, you may swing to the other extreme by always dominating conversations. Though you don't appear insecure, it is actually because of insecurity that you crave the spotlight and seek to elevate yourself so people might think more highly of you.

Could the "masks" we wear be fear too? We put up a façade so no one sees who we really are. We project an image that we are strong and life is great, but inside we are dying and feel alone. Instead of receiving the love and help we need, we pretend, keeping distance from others and God.

Regardless of how fear shows itself in your life, the bottom line is that fear fractures relationships. And when relationships are fractured, love is not present. Following this logic, fear and love cannot coexist, which means those in the grips of fear cannot love.

Saying we are unable to love when we fear seems strong, but it is fear that drives a wedge between us and other people and leaves us empty, immature, and incomplete. And in your emptiness, you can't give to others because you are only looking to be filled. As we learned when studying "idols," no human relationship or anything else can fill us. Only his perfect love can fill us, mature us, and make us complete.

Only his love for you has the power to drive out the fears that keep you from connected, secure, and loving relationships. As this love, which is found in knowing who he is and what he did for you, becomes the basis for your security, the fear that has kept you from boldly loving others and allowing yourself to be loved will begin to fade.

Now, instead of stressing over whether someone may not like you, you know you will be okay—there is no need to manipulate to get approval. Now instead of dictating the plans for your group, you can enjoy the evening when someone else's suggestion is taken over yours. Now instead of feeling unloved when you don't get asked to the dance, you do not fixate on whether something is wrong with you. Now instead of feeling rejected if you lose a Student Council election or someone forgets your birthday, you don't fall apart. Now, when you are "full of God," you won't have a fearful demanding heart.

Now when his love consumes you, it frees you!

DAY THREE _____
Straight to My Heart

Before answering the questions, reread the Scripture, being mindful of insights from the first two days.

:: What fears do you have in regards to how you relate to others?

:: How does fear show itself in your life (e.g., isolation, self-protection, insecurities, masks)?

:: Why is it impossible to love others when we are gripped by fear?

DAY FOUR   _____

Back to the Word

Reread the Scripture one more time and then take your time answering the questions below.

:: How is God's love the vehicle for driving out fears?

:: How does being full of fear or full of God affect your relationships positively or negatively?

:: How has realizing your own fears challenged or affected you this week?

DAY FIVE _____

Journaling and Prayer

:: Why does the Scripture tell us we cannot love God if we do not love our brother? Have you ever thought about your love of others being the outer expression of your love for God? Or how your lack of love toward others is a reflection of your vertical relationship to God?

Write out your thoughts.

Prayer

Lord, remind me constantly of your great love for me so that I move toward others in love, not away from them out of fear.

Week 43

Servant Love

DAY ONE
Straight from the Word

Read the Scripture and then follow the instructions below.

:: Philippians 2:1–15

[1] So if there is any encouragement in Christ, any comfort from love, any participation in the Spirit, any affection and sympathy, [2] complete my joy by being of the same mind, having the same love, being in full accord and of one mind. [3] Do nothing from selfish ambition or conceit, but in humility count others more significant than yourselves. [4] Let each of you look not only to his own interests, but also to the interests of others. [5] Have this mind among yourselves, which is yours in Christ Jesus, [6] who, though he was in the form of God, did not count equality with God a thing to be grasped, [7] but emptied himself, by taking the form of a servant, being born in the likeness of men. [8] And being found in human form, he humbled himself by becoming obedient to the point of death, even death on a cross. [9] Therefore God has highly exalted him and bestowed on him the name that is above every name, [10] so that at the name of Jesus every knee should bow, in heaven and on earth and under the earth, [11] and every tongue confess that Jesus Christ is Lord, to the glory of God the Father. . . . [14] Do all things without grumbling or disputing, [15] that you may be blameless and

innocent, children of God without blemish in the midst of a crooked and twisted generation, among whom you shine as lights in the world.

:: Underline what you see about Christ.

:: What commands are given for us?

:: What connection do you see between the commands and who Christ is?

:: Write down any thoughts or questions.

DAY TWO

The Word Applied

Your teacher assigned a group project, and the person you are paired with drives you crazy. Everything about him annoys you, and you especially have no patience with his long-winded ramblings. How are you going to manage working side by side for the next couple of weeks?

How is it possible to love this person the way Christ calls you to love?

We've studied what it means to be set apart, sent on a mission, to be imitators, to walk in love, and to display Christ. Have you noticed the common theme? In each of these recent passages along with the command to do something is the reminder of what Jesus did for you. If you already know what he did, why is it continually restated?

Because none of these commands are possible apart from resting in God's great love for you through the work of Jesus. We quickly forget and go back to thinking we can do it by our own human effort if we just try harder. But just as you need God's intervening grace to help you work with your assigned partner, we need to see that it is always his grace and the Spirit working in us that we ever do what is pleasing to him.

Only the gospel can motivate us to move toward others in love. This is why the Bible continually points us back to the gospel. Over and over again, we must hear of Jesus's love demonstrated in his life and death so that it recaptures our heart. If we hear a command without it being tied to the gospel, we think we are capable and sufficient to meet it on our own. We lose sight of the fact that only by God's grace can we obey and abide. And before you know it, we may be serving others, but our heart is puffed up by how good we think we are doing at meeting God's commands.

This week's passage reminds us that even Jesus, being equal to God and due all of his glory, took on the form of a servant. It is amazing and we gloss right over it! The King of the universe left his throne in heaven and came to earth as a human to live among sinners. He suffered humiliation, torture, and abandonment so that we could have eternal life.

Yet unlike Jesus, in our pride we think we are above doing certain tasks. And if we do them, we want the recognition for it. I am not even talking about major things, but daily life—like putting your dirty dishes away, picking up your trash off the floor so your mom doesn't have to, or scooping the dog poop in the backyard without being asked. It could be offering to give up your Friday night to babysit your younger siblings so your parents can have a night out, or letting your brother have the last piece of cake. It could be hanging clothes back up after trying them on in the dressing room instead of leaving an inside-out pile on the floor for the sales associate.

Having a servant's attitude is considering others' good over your own. This requires taking your eyes off yourself and realizing the world does not revolve around you. It goes back to our mission to glorify God by displaying Jesus to those around us. It means looking to Jesus not as an example of a humble servant, but as THE humble servant who stooped beneath you, took on all your sin, and then extended to you all of his glory! He had everything but gave it all up for your sake. Be filled with that reality and go serve!

DAY THREE
Straight to My Heart

Before answering the questions, reread the Scripture, being mindful of insights from the first two days.

:: What happens when you disconnect the gospel from any of God's commands for right living?

:: Why is Jesus not merely an example of how to live?

:: How does Jesus laying aside his glory and leaving heaven to take on the form of a servant impact you?

DAY FOUR _____

Back to the Word

Reread the Scripture one more time and then take your time answering the questions below.

:: How have you failed to love and serve others by not considering their good over your own?

:: In what specific ways can the gospel impact you daily in how you consider, love, and serve others?

:: Spend some time praying, asking God to cause the truths of the gospel to lead you to a greater love of those around you.

DAY FIVE   _____

Journaling and Prayer

:: Jesus is the light of the world, and as his children and image bearers we shine his light into the world. How are you imaging his light in the world? In what ways do you desire to shine brighter?

Spend time writing your thoughts.

Prayer

Lord, by your grace help me think less of myself and be more mindful of how to better love others.

Week 44

Controlling Kingdoms

DAY ONE

Straight from the Word

Read the Scripture and then follow the instructions below.

:: Ephesians 5:1–14

[1] Therefore be imitators of God, as beloved children. [2] And walk in love, as Christ loved us and gave himself up for us, a fragrant offering and sacrifice to God. [3] But sexual immorality and all impurity or covetousness must not even be named among you, as is proper among saints. [4] Let there be no filthiness nor foolish talk nor crude joking, which are out of place, but instead let there be thanksgiving. [5] For you may be sure of this, that everyone who is sexually immoral or impure, or who is covetous (that is, an idolater), has no inheritance in the kingdom of Christ and God. [6] Let no one deceive you with empty words, for because of these things the wrath of God comes upon the sons of disobedience. [7] Therefore do not become partners with them; [8] for at one time you were darkness, but now you are light in the Lord. Walk as children of light [9] (for the fruit of light is found in all that is good and right and true), [10] and try to discern what is pleasing to the Lord. [11] Take no part in the unfruitful works of darkness, but instead expose them. [12] For it is

shameful even to speak of the things that they do in secret. [13] But when anything is exposed by the light, it becomes visible, [14] for anything that becomes visible is light. Therefore it says, "Awake, O sleeper, and arise from the dead, and Christ will shine on you."

:: Circle the repetitive key words.

:: What is being contrasted in this passage?

:: Why is exposure of sin a good thing?

:: Ephesians 5:1–2 is our memory verse for Part III. Write it out below and begin memorizing it.

DAY TWO

The Word Applied

Whose kingdom are you living for? Is it *thy* kingdom come or *my* kingdom come?

One moment we joyfully sacrifice for someone else, and the next moment sinful selfish desires sneak in and attack. The apostle Paul understands this tension and addresses his concern about what influences and controls our heart and desires.

We are called to be "imitators of God" and "to walk in love." However, if something else has greater influence in our lives, it will control who or what we image forth. Paul lists some of those contrary influences affecting our ability to walk in love. But we need to dig deeper to see our hearts' bent when we engage in these specific kinds of conduct and speech.

Let's start with sexual immorality—this includes any sexual activity outside of God's design for marriage between one man and one woman. Our culture says waiting to be with just one person after you are married is old-fashioned. The sinful desires of wanting immediate pleasure, satisfaction, self-confidence, or promise of love leads us to adopt this logic. So we buy the lie and give ourselves in varying ways to those who are not our spouse.

When you covet something your friend has, it becomes the ruling idol of your heart at that moment. You are consumed by it and can't even be happy for your friend who has it. You believe that whatever the idol is will bring you the attention, popularity, status, security, or whatever it is you want for yourself and not your friend.

Filthy, foolish talk, or crude joking doesn't take much explaining but needs evaluating to see why we talk this way. Do you make fun of someone to feel like you are above or better than them? Do you share inappropriate humor with a group to feel cool? Do you dominate conversation, telling story after story, because of the attention it brings you? In each instance—whose kingdom are you concerned with?

Self is the common denominator in each of these named behaviors. All are self-seeking, self-gratifying, and take from others, which is in direct opposition to the self-sacrificial, giving love we are called to.

All these behaviors point deeper to the controlling desires ruling your heart—desires to live for your own kingdom, not God's.

Imitating him requires revolving your life around others, putting their interests ahead of your own, and thinking about how they feel and not what you want. But without the gospel driving you, other controlling influences will reign. The only way to combat them is to see again his sacrificial love for you.

Through the Word, God influences, controls, strengthens, and fills you to the point of being able to live for him and others. Remember that without the truths of the gospel (putting on the "armor"), we are left vulnerable to attack. Living in enemy territory with contrary influences makes proper protection absolutely essential. Guard yourself with gospel truth so that you may imitate him and walk in love toward others.

DAY THREE

Straight to My Heart

Before answering the questions, reread the Scripture, being mindful of insights from the first two days.

:: What new light has this lesson shed on Paul's listed behaviors?

:: Why must you look underneath the behavior to evaluate the desire driving all that you do?

:: How is it even possible to imitate God?

DAY FOUR
Back to the Word

:: Reread the Scripture passage and then continue working on memorizing Ephesians 5:1–2. When you think you have it, write it out below.

:: What are some specific ways you are being called to walk in love toward those in your life?

:: Why is it hard to walk in love, and where do you need help?

DAY FIVE

Journaling and Prayer

:: We know who God is not by sight, but from his Word. List
some of his characteristics you have seen throughout this
book study. How do you see yourself being an imitator?
How are you not?

Spend time writing your thoughts.

Prayer

*Lord, motivate me by your love to live for your kingdom and the
good of others and not be driven by self.*

Week 45

Friendship Foundations

DAY ONE
Straight from the Word

Read the Scriptures and then follow the instructions below.

Note: The John 15 passage is Jesus stressing the priority of abiding in him and his love for us. This leads to our loving one another.

:: John 15:9–17

[9] "As the Father has loved me, so have I loved you. Abide in my love. [10] If you keep my commandments, you will abide in my love, just as I have kept my Father's commandments and abide in his love. [11] These things I have spoken to you, that my joy may be in you, and that your joy may be full. [12] This is my commandment, that you love one another as I have loved you. [13] Greater love has no one than this, that someone lay down his life for his friends. [14] You are my friends if you do what I command you. [15] No longer do I call you servants, for the servant does not know what his master is doing; but I have called you friends, for all that I have heard from my Father I have made known to you. [16] You did not choose me, but I chose you and appointed you that you should go and bear fruit and that your fruit should abide, so that whatever you ask the Father in my name, he may give it to you. [17] These things I command you, so that you will love one another."

:: Proverbs 17:17

A friend loves at all times, and a brother is born for adversity.

:: Ecclesiastes 4:9–10

⁹ Two are better than one, because they have a good reward for their toil. ¹⁰ For if they fall, one will lift up his fellow. But woe to him who is alone when he falls and has not another to lift him up!

:: What do these verses say about friendship?

:: Underline the commandments given to us.

:: How can we keep these commands?

:: What strikes you about Jesus's friendship to us?

DAY TWO

The Word Applied

Your friend Riley did something that sparks school-wide gossip. As the story spreads, it becomes so exaggerated it's hard to know what really happened. But judgments are made and your group wants to disassociate themselves from Riley. You are torn. You know Riley messed up, but is it right to desert your friend?

The Bible has a lot to say about friendship. Think back to one of the first lessons in this book when we saw the Trinity revolving around one another. Then God declared it was not good for man to be alone so Eve was created for Adam. Like the Trinity, they imaged and displayed God to one another. Being created in his image, we were also made for relationships and to revolve our lives around each other.

But as you know sinners called to display Christ to other sinners is no easy task. Actually, it's impossible apart from God's grace and love bearing fruit in our lives. Starting with the John 15 passage, Jesus commands us to love one another as he has loved us.

As he loved us! We were his enemies yet he loved us with his life; his love was set on us from eternity past and there is nothing we can do to undo it. There are no conditions. God does not say, "if only he hadn't committed that sin" or "she needs to prove she loves me" or "he doesn't deserve my blessings." Too often our love toward other people is conditional with all sorts of "ifs, ands, and buts," which shows how unlike Christ we really are.

Because we won't ever love like he does, it's more than just saying we need to follow his example. We need him to love others through us. Going back to the situation with Riley—you can see how challenging it is to love someone, even a friend, when there is trouble. We would rather distance ourselves, sever the friendship, and move on. Who wants to get mixed up in someone else's problems, or, even worse, their sin?

But our next passages remind us that "a friend loves at all times," and adversity is when a friendship is really solidified. It is easy to be a friend when all is going well, there is no conflict, and you are similar to one another. But turn Riley's story around and consider for a moment that you are Riley. Think how differently you would feel about those who stick with you through the hard times. You would be so grateful those friends chose not to listen to the gossip and judge accordingly, but out of sincere love came to you directly. They perhaps sacrificed their own reputation by showing allegiance to you. They may have spoken truth in love that gave the hope you needed to make it through the days. They helped you up and pointed you back to Christ when you had fallen down. As a result, a much closer transparent friendship will be forged.

The loyal love of a friend is the foundation on which all our friendships should be built. It is the standard Jesus commanded, yet we cannot perfectly keep. But Jesus met that standard, and out of his abounding loving-kindness and loyal love laid down his life for sinners like you and me. Now by his grace we can be faithful friends.

DAY THREE _____

Straight to My Heart

Before answering the questions, reread the Scripture, being mindful of insights from the first two days.

:: How are you challenged by this lesson to view your friendships?

:: How can you be the kind of friend Jesus commands?

:: In the given situation, how could you walk alongside Riley as a true friend?

DAY FOUR   _____

Back to the Word

Reread the Scripture one more time and then take your time answering the questions below.

:: How have the hurts you experienced in friendship led to greater empathy and love or contributed to a hardened heart and withdrawal?

:: In what ways do the truths of this lesson challenge you to be a true friend even when you have been mistreated?

:: To whom in your life can you be that loyal friend and what would that look like?

DAY FIVE _____

Journaling and Prayer

:: How do the verses from this week's reading convict you? How do they encourage or inspire you?

Spend time writing your thoughts.

Prayer

Lord, thank you for laying your life down for a sinful friend like me. By your grace teach me to be a true friend.

Week 46

A True Friend

DAY ONE
Straight from the Word

Read the Scriptures and then follow the instructions below.

:: 1 Samuel 18:1–9

¹ As soon as he had finished speaking to Saul, the soul of Jonathan was knit to the soul of David, and Jonathan loved him as his own soul. ² And Saul took him that day and would not let him return to his father's house. ³ Then Jonathan made a covenant with David, because he loved him as his own soul. ⁴ And Jonathan stripped himself of the robe that was on him and gave it to David, and his armor, and even his sword and his bow and his belt. ⁵ And David went out and was successful wherever Saul sent him, so that Saul set him over the men of war. And this was good in the sight of all the people and also in the sight of Saul's servants. ⁶ As they were coming home, when David returned from striking down the Philistine, the women came out of all the cities of Israel, singing and dancing, to meet King Saul, with tambourines, with songs of joy, and with musical instruments. ⁷ And the women sang to one another as they celebrated, "Saul has struck down his thousands, and David his ten thousands." ⁸ And Saul was very angry, and this saying displeased him. He said, "They have ascribed to David ten thousands, and to me they have ascribed thousands, and

what more can he have but the kingdom?" [9] And Saul eyed David from that day on.

:: 1 Samuel 19:1–5

[1] And Saul spoke to Jonathan his son and to all his servants, that they should kill David. But Jonathan, Saul's son, delighted much in David. [2] And Jonathan told David, "Saul my father seeks to kill you. Therefore be on your guard in the morning. Stay in a secret place and hide yourself. [3] And I will go out and stand beside my father in the field where you are, and I will speak to my father about you. And if I learn anything I will tell you." [4] And Jonathan spoke well of David to Saul his father and said to him, "Let not the king sin against his servant David, because he has not sinned against you, and because his deeds have brought good to you. [5] For he took his life in his hand and he struck down the Philistine, and the LORD worked a great salvation for all Israel. You saw it, and rejoiced. Why then will you sin against innocent blood by killing David without cause?"

:: Make five observations about Jonathan's friendship toward David.

:: How did Jonathan make David great at his own expense?

:: Why did Saul want to kill David?

:: Write down any thoughts or questions.

DAY TWO

The Word Applied

How likely are you to allow someone to go ahead of you in a long line you've been waiting in? What about your willingness to go late to a friend's party so you can support your little brother in his game? Even if you do oblige, do you complain about it?

This week's text is the story of sacrifice made between Jonathan and David, who may be history's most famous faithful friends. We shouldn't overlook the fact that Jonathan was to be the king after his father Saul. As was customary and still true in monarchies today, the firstborn son inherits the throne and becomes king when his father dies. As Jonathan stripped off his robes and made the covenant with David, he handed David his right to the kingship!

Who does that? Even in small, insignificant ways we are unwilling to sacrifice. But here Jonathan gives up being the next king and all the power that goes with it! As we saw last week, being a loyal friend may incur a cost. In Jonathan's case, his promise to David cost him his kingship, but also the love of his father. His father had become jealous of David and wanted to kill him. Yet, despite the conflict this brought into Jonathan's life, his understanding of covenant drove his commitment to his relationship with David.

In the Old Testament, covenants were binding oaths, a promise that if broken meant death to the offender. Sometimes this was between God and man, like the covenant to Abraham extending to all his children; other times it was between people, like with Jonathan and David. For us, living in a world where marriage vows and legal contracts are routinely broken, it is hard to grasp the permanency of a covenant relationship.

This negotiable mentality shows in our lack of commitment and faithfulness. Just consider the reason you may tend to be noncommittal about plans. Are you waiting to see what better options might come? Or think about when you are more concerned with checking your phone than listening to the person you are sitting next to. Indirectly you are communicating that they are not as important to you.

A flippant approach to friendship leaves us doubting our value. We wonder if we will be ditched, listened to, cared for, or supported. We fear that in opening up we may be gossiped about, laughed at, or misunderstood, so our relationships stay at a surface level.

David knew that Jonathan had his back and was even willing to die for him. While this can make us feel guilty about how much we fail in loving others, the picture portrayed by Jonathan and David is a pointer to the way Jesus loves you. He is a covenant-keeping King who loves to give richly. He is a King who gave up his throne in heaven and felt the sting of his Father's wrath. He is a King who stripped himself of his righteous robes and died so that you could be clothed in his perfect majesty.

What a true friend we have in Jesus!

DAY THREE
Straight to My Heart

Before answering the questions, reread the Scripture, being mindful of insights from the first two days.

:: How should understanding covenant as described in yesterday's lesson shape your view of relationships?

:: How do you see Christ pictured in the story of Jonathan and David?

:: Why is it important to understand and remember Christ is the only perfect true friend?

DAY FOUR
Back to the Word

Reread the Scripture one more time and then take your time answering the questions below.

:: What did you see about loyalty through the story of David and Jonathan?

:: In what way does this lesson cause you to reevaluate the type of friend you are to others?

:: What do you need to confess and repent in regard to how you have treated others?

DAY FIVE

Journaling and Prayer

:: Have you approached your friendships as a covenant or as a consumer? Are you more concerned with yourself and how you benefit from the relationship? Or do you seek the best interests of your friends? Write about how you can be a better true friend.

Prayer

Lord, thank you for being the perfect promise-keeper. Help me in my relationships to remember what it means to live in covenant with one another.

Week 47

Bearing Burdens

DAY ONE

Straight from the Word

Read the Scripture and then follow the instructions below.

:: Galatians 6:1–10, 14

[1] Brothers, if anyone is caught in any transgression, you who are spiritual should restore him in a spirit of gentleness. Keep watch on yourself, lest you too be tempted. [2] Bear one another's burdens, and so fulfill the law of Christ. [3] For if anyone thinks he is something, when he is nothing, he deceives himself. [4] But let each one test his own work, and then his reason to boast will be in himself alone and not in his neighbor. [5] For each will have to bear his own load. [6] Let the one who is taught the word share all good things with the one who teaches. [7] Do not be deceived: God is not mocked, for whatever one sows, that will he also reap. [8] For the one who sows to his own flesh will from the flesh reap corruption, but the one who sows to the Spirit will from the Spirit reap eternal life. [9] And let us not grow weary of doing good, for in due season we will reap, if we do not give up. [10] So then, as we have opportunity, let us do good to everyone, and especially to those who are of the household of faith.

[14] But far be it from me to boast except in the cross of our Lord Jesus Christ, by which the world has been crucified to me, and I to the world.

:: What temptation could easily creep in when trying to help someone in sin?

:: What does "sows to his own flesh" mean?

:: How would you summarize this passage?

:: Galatians 6:14 is another great memory verse. Work on memorizing it.

DAY TWO

The Word Applied

Alex has stopped hanging out with your group of friends and has gotten caught up in a wild crowd using drugs and alcohol. You have been best friends since meeting at church when you were little, and you miss the old Alex and hate that now you barely even talk. Then one day Alex catches you off guard at your locker. She is distraught and confides in you that at a weekend party she got high and vaguely remembers having sex before passing out. While the details are a blur, she now feels used and taken advantage of.

Your emotions are all over the place. You are angry someone did this to her while at the same time think she shouldn't be so surprised considering her behavior. With all her troubles and new "druggie" reputation, you want to distance yourself from her, but she is crying for help and has come to you. What should you do?

Galatians 6 is written for you. It is a command and warning given not to the ones burdened but to those called to help. The body of Christ, the church, is to serve as the ER nurses who lift, carry, support, mend, and help those who are wounded, in order to restore them gently back to health. No matter what the burdens are, we are called to bear them. We are called to be the hands and feet of Jesus by coming to the aid of those who are wounded, hurt, and broken because of their sin or because of the sin of others.

You don't need to look far to see the wounded—if it's not you, it's those all around you in your schools, neighborhoods, and churches. There are those fighting cancer, dealing with their parents' divorce, or struggling financially. Those who fear they will never measure up to other people's expectations. Those who think they have to go to drastic measures in order to feel attractive. Those whose sin or hurt have left them so numb that they have to cut themselves to feel alive. Those who struggle with such deep depression that suicide looks like a better option than life.

But here is the warning: pride can quickly overtake you who are called to help. The temptation will be to compare yourself to those who have fallen and to think you are better and more spiritual than they. Too easily you could begin to think you are better than those who are burdened because you are not struggling with the same thing or because you have not done the things they have to become wounded.

The only way you can help without making the broken feel inadequate or beneath you is by going to the cross. On the cross Jesus stooped to carry the weight of all our heavy burdens. It is where all our failures to love God and others were nailed to the One who never failed. It is the only place we can boast, and he is the only One who can give us the strength to help carry someone else's load. So by his power and grace, stoop beneath those near you who are hurting, regardless of the reason, and help lift the burden so they don't have to suffer alone.

DAY THREE

Straight to My Heart

Before answering the questions, reread the Scripture, being mindful of insights from the first two days.

:: What prevents you from getting involved with someone who needs a friend to bear their burdens?

:: How might pride or a judgmental attitude develop as you try to help someone in need?

:: What does it mean that we can only boast in the cross?

DAY FOUR

Back to the Word

:: Reread the Scripture passage and then continue memorizing Galatians 6:14. When you think you have it, write it below.

:: How can you help bear the burdens of a suffering friend or other broken person God has put in your path?

:: How can you keep from growing weary of doing good?

DAY FIVE

Journaling and Prayer

:: Think further about what it means to boast only in the cross of Jesus. How should this keep you humble? How does this motivate you to serve?

Write out your thoughts.

Prayer

Lord, only by your grace am I upheld. Stir compassion and love in me so that I am willing and able to bear the burdens of others, even when it is inconvenient and messy.

Week 48

Forgiveness

DAY ONE
Straight from the Word

Read the Scripture and then follow the instructions below.

Note: As Jesus gains popularity, the religious leaders grow more suspicious. For this reason Simon invites Jesus to his home to find out more about him.

:: Luke 7:36–48

36 One of the Pharisees asked him [Jesus] to eat with him, and he went into the Pharisee's house and reclined at the table. 37 And behold, a woman of the city, who was a sinner, when she learned that he was reclining at table in the Pharisee's house, brought an alabaster flask of ointment, 38 and standing behind him at his feet, weeping, she began to wet his feet with her tears and wiped them with the hair of her head and kissed his feet and anointed them with the ointment. 39 Now when the Pharisee who had invited him saw this, he said to himself, "If this man were a prophet, he would have known who and what sort of woman this is who is touching him, for she is a sinner." 40 And Jesus answering said to him, "Simon, I have something to say to you." And he answered, "Say it, Teacher."

41 "A certain moneylender had two debtors. One owed five hundred denarii, and the other fifty. 42 When they could not pay, he cancelled the debt of both. Now which of them will love him more?"

[43] Simon answered, "The one, I suppose, for whom he cancelled the larger debt." And he said to him, "You have judged rightly." [44] Then turning toward the woman he said to Simon, "Do you see this woman? I entered your house; you gave me no water for my feet, but she has wet my feet with her tears and wiped them with her hair. [45] You gave me no kiss, but from the time I came in she has not ceased to kiss my feet. [46] You did not anoint my head with oil, but she has anointed my feet with ointment. [47] Therefore I tell you, her sins, which are many, are forgiven—for she loved much. But he who is forgiven little, loves little." [48] And he said to her, "Your sins are forgiven."

:: List five things you learn about the woman in the story.

:: Why does Jesus tell the story about the moneylender to the Pharisee?

:: What does Jesus's parable reveal about the Pharisee and the woman?

:: Why does the woman love Jesus in a way the Pharisee does not?

DAY TWO
The Word Applied

Do you ever get annoyed if a friend pays more attention to a mere acquaintance than to you? Perhaps you have something to share with your friend and keep waiting for the right moment, but he or she is preoccupied with this other person. You grow impatient because clearly you are more important!

Those feelings may be similar to the Pharisee in our passage who is appalled that Jesus is not only paying attention to the town prostitute but allowing her to touch and anoint him with oil. Why in the world would Jesus give her the time of day—especially when it would make him unclean? Surely he must not know who she is, or he would send her away.

But Jesus knew exactly who she was. And he knew exactly what was going through the Pharisee's mind about her, which is exactly why he tells the story of the moneylender.

The story is one of many parables in the book of Luke. Jesus liked teaching with parables, which are short stories used to teach a deeper truth because of their ability to shoot an arrow straight to the heart of those listening. The hidden truth within a parable isn't at first always easily seen. Although the Pharisee correctly answered Jesus's question that the one with the larger debt cancelled would be more grateful, he doesn't understand Jesus's point.

The woman knows she is a messed-up guilty sinner in desperate need of a Savior. But the Pharisee doesn't see that he is also a messed-up guilty sinner in desperate need of a Savior.

That is why Jesus points out that how greatly you see your need of a Savior will determine how great grace is to you. If you view yourself as having it all together, grace won't change you.

The woman knew she needed forgiveness and grace; the Pharisee did not. The woman fell at Jesus's feet in worship of who he was; the Pharisee gave Jesus, who was his guest, no special treatment. The woman discovered that when her identity was found in Jesus, her label was no longer the needy, unlovable, or insecure one. The Pharisee, on the other hand, was still self-consumed, not seeing that he was truly needy, unlovable, and insecure!

Do you see the deeper truth? Not just for the Pharisee's sake, but for yours?

We miss being amazed by the gospel because we don't see how desperately we need forgiveness and grace. We appear to be good Christians on the outside, but neglect everything going on in our hearts—the idols and fears, the controlling influences and kingdom of self that nobody sees but God.

We need a Savior in the same way the prostitute needed a Savior. Failure to recognize we are all in need of forgiveness will limit our ability to extend grace and forgiveness to others. Forgiveness is not easy. Sometimes it is extremely painful, and it is always costly because it requires absorbing the debt someone else owes. But that is exactly what Christ did for you on the cross.

DAY THREE

Straight to My Heart

Before answering the questions, reread the Scripture, being mindful of insights from the first two days.

:: How do you identify with what the Pharisee was thinking?

:: What people or situations make holding a grudge easy and granting forgiveness hard?

:: How does this lesson challenge you in the area of forgiveness?

DAY FOUR
Back to the Word

Reread the Scripture one more time and then take your time answering the questions below.

:: What is the deeper truth this parable is teaching?

:: What do you see about yourself through the deeper truth of this parable?

:: Do you see that your need is as great as the prostitute's in the story? Why or why not?

DAY FIVE

Journaling and Prayer

:: Reflect on what the Lord has been teaching you this week about your need for forgiveness and grace. How have you been convicted or challenged? How have you seen your need to be amazed again by the gospel?

Prayer

Lord, help me see my need for forgiveness and by your grace be able to extend forgiveness to others.

Week 49

Real Repentance

DAY ONE

Straight from the Word

Read the Scripture and then follow the instructions below.

:: 2 Samuel 12:1–13

[1] And the LORD sent Nathan to David. He came to him and said to him, "There were two men in a certain city, the one rich and the other poor. [2] The rich man had very many flocks and herds, [3] but the poor man had nothing but one little ewe lamb, which he had bought. And he brought it up, and it grew up with him and with his children. It used to eat of his morsel and drink from his cup and lie in his arms, and it was like a daughter to him. [4] Now there came a traveler to the rich man, and he was unwilling to take one of his own flock or herd to prepare for the guest who had come to him, but he took the poor man's lamb and prepared it for the man who had come to him." [5] Then David's anger was greatly kindled against the man, and he said to Nathan, "As the LORD lives, the man who has done this deserves to die, [6] and he shall restore the lamb fourfold, because he did this thing, and because he had no pity."

[7] Nathan said to David, "You are the man! Thus says the LORD, the God of Israel, 'I anointed you king over Israel, and I delivered you out of the hand of Saul. [8] And I gave you your master's house and your

master's wives into your arms and gave you the house of Israel and of Judah. And if this were too little, I would add to you as much more. [9] Why have you despised the word of the LORD, to do what is evil in his sight? You have struck down Uriah the Hittite with the sword and have taken his wife to be your wife and have killed him with the sword of the Ammonites. [10] Now therefore the sword shall never depart from your house, because you have despised me and have taken the wife of Uriah the Hittite to be your wife.' [11] Thus says the LORD, 'Behold, I will raise up evil against you out of your own house. And I will take your wives before your eyes and give them to your neighbor, and he shall lie with your wives in the sight of this sun. [12] For you did it secretly, but I will do this thing before all Israel and before the sun.'" [13] David said to Nathan, "I have sinned against the LORD." And Nathan said to David, "The LORD also has put away your sin; you shall not die.

:: How did God use Nathan in David's life?

:: What made Nathan's role extra hard? Think about who David was!

:: How did David respond?

:: Who did David understand his sin to be primarily against?

DAY TWO _____
The Word Applied

Morgan was worried about her friend Allison. Normally very outgo-
ing and fun, now she was withdrawn, regularly backing out of social
plans, and hardly eating. Morgan feared she might be struggling with
an eating disorder. She wanted to reach out to Allison but wasn't sure
what to say or do. What if she voiced her suspicion and it wasn't true?
Or what if it was true but Allison denied it and hated Morgan for
asking?

Will has secretly used anabolic steroids to build muscle mass.
His sudden superior athletic performance along with his chiseled
six-pack, deepened voice, and acne made Cooper suspicious. Cooper
has already seen firsthand the effect of prolonged steroid use on his
brother's health, so he knows he can't let his friend continue down this
same path. But what should he say to help Will see and turn from his
sinful idols?

To confront a friend in sin is never easy, but sometimes it is the
necessary action God calls us to after seeking wisdom and praying
much. This was the scary situation Nathan faced when God sent him
to probe the powerful King David in regards to having his friend
Uriah murdered to conceal the affair with his wife, Bathsheba.

Nathan's goal was to lead David to repentance and restoration;
therefore, his approach was not condemnation and attack. This did

not mean glossing over the sin, but communicating in a gentle manner so as not to put David on the defense. Because of the love and grace demonstrated, David saw that not only was Nathan for him, but God was too. Finally he felt free to own up to his sin, which is the first step to healing and restoration.

True repentance like his is not simply a confession of sin because you are sorry you got caught and now have to deal with the consequences. It is not just being sorry because you look bad or hurt someone. It is more than a general acknowledgment of being a sinner.

True repentance requires owning your sin in order to disown it, so it doesn't own you. Only honest, specific acknowledgment and growing hatred of your sin leads to true heart change. With that comes a greater sorrow over grieving God than caring about saving face. David was able to see his sin as not just breaking the "law," but as a turning away from the love of God and toward something else—to see his sin as ultimately against God.

God's love for you is so great and complete that he turned down the prayer of his own Son and let him hang on a cross to cover all of your sins—not just past sins, but those you don't even know you will commit, and the recurring sins you seem to give in to no matter how many times you confess.

When Morgan decided to write Allison a letter about her concerns, she prefaced it with what a special friend Allison has been. The tone of the letter was grace that spoke the truth and love of Jesus that Allison needed to hear. Cooper, too, risked his friendship to confront Will, and even though Will rejected him, Cooper was at peace knowing his intent was sincere love for Will. With Allison's sin exposed, freedom and true repentance began to take hold of her life, while Cooper continued to trust in the intervening work of the Holy Spirit to convict Will in his timing.

DAY THREE

Straight to My Heart

Before answering the questions, reread the Scripture, being mindful of insights from the first two days.

:: What keeps you from confession and repentance?

:: What is true repentance and what is it not?

:: How was Nathan able to help David see his sin?

DAY FOUR _____

Back to the Word

Reread the Scripture one more time and then take your time answering the questions below.

:: What does it mean to need "Nathans" in our lives and to be Nathans to others?

:: Why do you think our sin is first and foremost against God and not other people?

DAY FIVE

Journaling and Prayer

:: What would keep you from being a Nathan to someone? What would the fear be? What might be the consequences? Would you be a true friend if you let them continue in sin? Why would the risk be worth it? Would someone be a true friend to you if they let you continue in your sin? How do you think you would respond if someone came to you as a Nathan?

Prayer

Lord, may I be quick to see my sin as primarily against you. And by your love enable me to be a Nathan to another if I need to be and to respond with gratitude should someone need to be a Nathan to me.

Week 50

Christian Clothes

DAY ONE

Straight from the Word

Read the Scripture and then follow the instructions below.

:: Colossians 3:1–17

¹ If then you have been raised with Christ, seek the things that are above, where Christ is, seated at the right hand of God. ² Set your minds on things that are above, not on things that are on earth. ³ For you have died, and your life is hidden with Christ in God. ⁴ When Christ who is your life appears, then you also will appear with him in glory.

⁵ Put to death therefore what is earthly in you: sexual immorality, impurity, passion, evil desire, and covetousness, which is idolatry. ⁶ On account of these the wrath of God is coming. ⁷ In these you too once walked, when you were living in them. ⁸ But now you must put them all away: anger, wrath, malice, slander, and obscene talk from your mouth. ⁹ Do not lie to one another, seeing that you have put off the old self with its practices ¹⁰ and have put on the new self, which is being renewed in knowledge after the image of its creator. ¹¹ Here there is not Greek and Jew, circumcised and uncircumcised, barbarian, Scythian, slave, free; but Christ is all, and in all.

¹² Put on then, as God's chosen ones, holy and beloved, compassionate hearts, kindness, humility, meekness, and patience, ¹³ bearing

with one another and, if one has a complaint against another, forgiving each other; as the Lord has forgiven you, so you also must forgive. [14] And above all these put on love, which binds everything together in perfect harmony. [15] And let the peace of Christ rule in your hearts, to which indeed you were called in one body. And be thankful. [16] Let the word of Christ dwell in you richly, teaching and admonishing one another in all wisdom, singing psalms and hymns and spiritual songs, with thankfulness in your hearts to God. [17] And whatever you do, in word or deed, do everything in the name of the Lord Jesus, giving thanks to God the Father through him.

:: Underline the commands given in the passage.

:: Where does our motivation and ability to keep these commands come from?

:: What "clothing" is the most important to put on?

:: Write down your thoughts about the connection of thankfulness in this passage.

DAY TWO
The Word Applied

What do you do when you have a crush on somebody? Do you creep on his or her social media pages? Take a different route to class so you "accidentally" bump in to each other? Do you spend extra time getting ready so you look your best?

The idea of "love" drives such behavior. *Love* is used loosely here because true love known in marriage is not at all the same as the infatuation of a crush or a girlfriend/boyfriend relationship. But for the sake of the example, you see how love changes us and influences what we do.

This passage reminds the Christian of the extent of God's love—the fact that he has chosen you to be the special recipient of his particular love, the gift of his Son. God actually looks upon and loves the Christian the exact same way he looks upon and loves his Son!

When this love sinks in to your soul, you will change. No longer will the ways of your old self have the same appeal. You will care about new things. His love drives and transforms you to be compassionate, kind, humble, gentle, and patient.

These are the "clothes" of a Christian. We can "put on" these clothes because they are Christ's clothes that he has already put on us through his Spirit living in us. Here is what I mean:

> Christ is compassionate toward you in the way he looks upon you in your sin and does not reject you but extends grace. Now you are commanded to wear his compassion toward others.

> Christ is kind toward you in the way he sees your helplessness and continues to give immeasurably more than you ask or imagine. Now you are commanded to wear his kindness for others.

> Christ humbled himself by stooping to take on flesh to identify with you and suffer for you. Now you are commanded to wear his humility by stooping and identifying with others.

Christ is gentle toward you in not treating you as your sins deserve. Now you are commanded to wear his gentleness and not treat each other harshly.

Christ is patient with you by putting up with your ongoing sin and rebellion against him. Now you are commanded to wear his patience with others who sin against you.

Christ has passed down his clothes and put them on you. And though it sounds like five different garments, it is really just one—love. The love of Christ is what transforms you to represent and reflect him to others. It is what enables you to bear, endure, and put up with one another. It is what leads you to forgive others the way God has forgiven you. When Christ is everything to you, his love, his peace, and his Word will rule your heart and govern how you live toward others.

DAY THREE _____
Straight to My Heart

Before answering the questions, reread the Scripture, being mindful of insights from the first two days.

:: Why is being captivated by Christ's love the binding component to how compassionate, kind, humble, gentle, or patient any of us are?

:: When you see that you are not wearing your Christian clothes and your "old self" reemerges, what do you need?

:: How have you seen the effects of Christ's transforming love on your life?

DAY FOUR _____

Back to the Word

Reread the Scripture one more time and then take your time answering the questions below.

:: Is compassion, kindness, humility, gentleness, or patience the hardest for you? Why do you think this is the case?

:: To who in your life—and in what ways—can you show more compassion, kindness, humility, gentleness, and patience?

:: Pray right now for each of these people and ask God to grant you opportunities to love them better.

DAY FIVE

Journaling and Prayer

:: Colossians 3:16 says, "Let the word of Christ dwell in you richly." What is that word we need to constantly meditate on? Why is that? What evidence do you see or not see of it dwelling richly in you?

Write out your thoughts.

Prayer

Lord, I want to be clothed in compassion, kindness, humility, gentleness, and patience. Help me to "wear" these clothes and reflect you to those around me.

Week 51

True Discipleship

DAY ONE

Straight from the Word

Read the Scripture and then follow the instructions below.

:: Mark 8:27–38

27 And Jesus went on with his disciples to the villages of Caesarea Philippi. And on the way he asked his disciples, "Who do people say that I am?" 28 And they told him, "John the Baptist; and others say, Elijah; and others, one of the prophets." 29 And he asked them, "But who do you say that I am?" Peter answered him, "You are the Christ." 30 And he strictly charged them to tell no one about him. 31 And he began to teach them that the Son of Man must suffer many things and be rejected by the elders and the chief priests and the scribes and be killed, and after three days rise again. 32 And he said this plainly. And Peter took him aside and began to rebuke him. 33 But turning and seeing his disciples, he rebuked Peter and said, "Get behind me, Satan! For you are not setting your mind on the things of God, but on the things of man." 34 And calling the crowd to him with his disciples, he said to them, "If anyone would come after me, let him deny himself and take up his cross and follow me. 35 For whoever would save his life will lose it, but whoever loses his life for my sake and the gospel's will save it. 36 For what does it profit a man to gain the whole world and forfeit his

soul? [37] For what can a man give in return for his soul? [38] For whoever is ashamed of me and of my words in this adulterous and sinful generation, of him will the Son of Man also be ashamed when he comes in the glory of his Father with the holy angels."

:: Make five observations from the passage.

:: Why did the Son of Man have to suffer, be rejected and crucified?

:: How was Peter setting his mind on the things of men and not the things of God?

:: Underline what Christ says is the mark of a true disciple.

DAY TWO

The Word Applied

Most people equate denying with depriving, like giving up chocolate for Lent. Or thinking they must give up their possessions, bad habits, or modern conveniences. While there may be times you are called to give up some of those things, denying yourself is something more—it is to deny *Self*.

Denying self is what Jesus says marks a true disciple. But our self-addiction causes us to kick and scream if anything denies us the happiness we think we deserve. We live as if we can order our days to our liking even though Scripture clearly states our lives are not our own. A true disciple, however, understands that King Jesus rules over him or her. He is the one who orders, controls, and ordains all things. And more often than not, what he deems "good" looks completely different than what we would choose.

So we may give it a spiritual spin and say our disability, injury, hardship, or trial is our "cross to bear," meaning a small price to pay for the sake of Christ. But this is not the extent of what Jesus meant. No, taking up your cross is Jesus's demand to die to your own pursuits and live instead for what God pursues—to give up your will for his will.

This may mean giving your hard-earned money to someone in need instead of spending it on what you were saving toward. It could mean dropping an extracurricular activity to free your time for serving. It might mean accepting a lower grade for late homework because it was more important on a particular evening to console a friend than get your assignment done.

To follow Jesus means that he leads and you submit to his leadership, that you live for his glory as more important than your own. Because his kingdom is more important than your kingdom, you devote yourself to his.

If these are the demands of discipleship, are you sure you want to be a disciple?

Well, here is the surprise—you can't meet those demands! No one can. No one is qualified to be his disciple. That is because the real disciple in this passage is actually Jesus. He is the only one who denied himself, who died to himself, and who lived devoted to God's glory.

We are actually like Peter in this passage, more concerned with keeping our life. And if we are honest, most of the time we are more concerned about living for our own glory and building our own kingdoms to Self. That is why Jesus had to suffer, and be rejected and killed.

Jesus traveled the road of true discipleship because we cannot. When you understand it is not about your devotion to him, but his devotion to you, then you will freely give up yourself, your life, and your will for him and count the loss as gain!

DAY THREE _____

Straight to My Heart

Before answering the questions, reread the Scripture, being mindful of insights from the first two days.

:: What does it mean to deny self?

:: How would you explain that to lose your life is really to save it?

:: What does it mean that Jesus is really the true disciple in the passage?

DAY FOUR _____

Back to the Word

Reread the Scripture one more time and then take your time answering the questions below.

:: When have you found yourself to be ashamed to speak up for Christ or to make known your beliefs?

:: In what situations or with which people is it most hard to die to your own desires?

:: Next time you are tempted to deny him (not stand strong for the gospel) or when you struggle to die to your own desires, how can seeing Jesus as the only true disciple help you?

DAY FIVE _____

Journaling and Prayer

:: Reflect on what Mark 8:36 means when it says, "For what does it profit a man to gain the whole world and forfeit his soul?"

Spend time writing your thoughts.

Prayer

Lord, thank you for living and dying devoted to me. Help me now to freely give of myself for others' good.

Week 52

Abiding in Christ

DAY ONE
Straight from the Word

Read the Scripture and then follow the instructions below.

:: John 15:1–17

[1] "I am the true vine, and my Father is the vinedresser. [2] Every branch in me that does not bear fruit he takes away, and every branch that does bear fruit he prunes, that it may bear more fruit. [3] Already you are clean because of the word that I have spoken to you. [4] Abide in me, and I in you. As the branch cannot bear fruit by itself, unless it abides in the vine, neither can you, unless you abide in me. [5] I am the vine; you are the branches. Whoever abides in me and I in him, he it is that bears much fruit, for apart from me you can do nothing. [6] If anyone does not abide in me he is thrown away like a branch and withers; and the branches are gathered, thrown into the fire, and burned. [7] If you abide in me, and my words abide in you, ask whatever you wish, and it will be done for you. [8] By this my Father is glorified, that you bear much fruit and so prove to be my disciples. [9] As the Father has loved me, so have I loved you. Abide in my love. [10] If you keep my commandments, you will abide in my love, just as I have kept my Father's commandments and abide in his love. [11] These things I have spoken to you, that my joy may be in you, and that your joy may be full.

¹² "This is my commandment, that you love one another as I have loved you. ¹³ Greater love has no one than this, that someone lay down his life for his friends. ¹⁴ You are my friends if you do what I command you. ¹⁵ No longer do I call you servants, for the servant does not know what his master is doing; but I have called you friends, for all that I have heard from my Father I have made known to you. ¹⁶ You did not choose me, but I chose you and appointed you that you should go and bear fruit and that your fruit should abide, so that whatever you ask the Father in my name, he may give it to you. ¹⁷ These things I command you, so that you will love one another."

:: Circle the key repetitive words.

:: Make five observations about the passage.

:: Explain what the vine and the branches word picture depicts.

:: How can we bear much fruit?

DAY TWO

The Word Applied

Since its 1988 inception, Nike's "Just Do It" campaign has become iconic, not just to the brand but in our culture. The tagline's motivational appeal spread well beyond the athletic realm and resonates with audiences in various contexts. As Christians we have bought into the "Just Do It" mind-set, adopting this approach to our Christian life. By this I mean that we think we need to just do more for God. We try to be more obedient. To love others better. To be more patient. To work on anger issues. To do all these things to be a better Christian.

How is that going for you? Do you start out energized, ready to tackle and achieve these goals, but before you know it have messed up? Do you beat yourself up and try harder? Do you try to hide the fact that you messed up? Do you struggle to get back on track and look to new techniques for help?

We need to take a closer look at the word *abide*. In our passage it appears eleven times, which makes it the key word and a good indicator of the main point. According to the *Merriam-Webster Dictionary*, *abide* means to "endure," "to remain in a stable or fixed state," or "to wait without yielding or giving in."[9] Applying that definition to Jesus's command to "abide in me" leaves us with one conclusion—our top priority is to abide in Jesus.

We are to continually endure and remain in him, to continually trust in his work and dependence on him. Only by staying connected to the life-giving Vine are we able to "bear the fruit" of displaying Christ. The problem is that without realizing it, we try to live the Christian life not connected to him, and we fall back into the "Just Do It" approach. When you do this, you slip back into fruit bearing as your priority and job, instead of *abiding* in him and his righteousness. You have forgotten that your strength and ability comes only from resting in who Jesus is and what he has done for you.

"Apart from me you can do nothing" means you can't maintain your relationship with him, you can't obey him, you can't bear fruit, and you don't even have the desire to do so apart from Jesus's provision. In your helplessness, Jesus wants you to ask for his help. He loves to hear the cries of his people admitting their need. Your prayers might go something like this:

Lord, give me the desire to spend time in your Word.
Strengthen my faith and help me trust you. Help
me abide in you. Draw me closer. Help me bear
good fruit. Help me not to get so angry. Help me
not to be so consumed with what other people think
about me. Help me to love others. Help me to dis-
play you.

To abide in him we must stop trying to fix ourselves, but fix our eyes on him. To abide in him we must be in the Word, and we must look for him in his Word. Remember all we have looked at over the course of this book. Remember the Bible is his story, not ours, so if we go to the Word like it's an instruction manual, we will miss the message of God's Word. From start to finish, Old Testament to New, it is about finding life in our Savior and King.

I hope this book has given you a greater understanding of who King Jesus is and why we must constantly hear the story of his love for his people. The gospel alone has the power to change people. I pray that this book has challenged you to find life by abiding in him alone!

DAY THREE _____

Straight to My Heart

Before answering the questions, reread the Scripture, being mindful of insights from the first two days.

:: Why should the "Just Do It" mind-set not be applied to Christianity?

:: In what ways have you seen this philosophy trickle into Christian teaching?

:: Why is abiding in him your highest priority?

DAY FOUR

Back to the Word

Reread the Scripture one more time and then take your time answering the questions below.

:: Through abiding in him, what fruit do you see or not yet see but desire?

:: When you are abiding in him and finding life in the finished work of Jesus on your behalf, how does your life look differently than when you are not abiding in him?

:: Why is abiding in him still hard?

DAY FIVE _____
Journaling and Prayer

:: You have just completed an entire year in this book. How has your understanding of the gospel changed or deepened? Who do you now know Christ to be that you didn't before? How has this affected your thoughts, struggles, and relationships?

Spend time writing your thoughts.

Prayer

Lord, thank you for your Word. Thank you for loving me to the uttermost and upholding me in all things. Help me to abide in you so my life will be wrapped up in your story.

Acknowledgments

This book has been bottled in my head far too long, so my biggest thank-you goes to my husband, Pete. Without you I wouldn't have much content! Your sermons and teaching have been pivotal to my own understanding, growth, and the writing of this devotional. Your encouragement has given me the confidence I needed for teaching and writing. By helping me organize my thoughts and the direction of this book, I was finally able to productively write instead of staring at a blank computer screen. Then when it came to the content editing, you graciously spent our nineteenth anniversary and a good part of the rest of the week talking me through changes. Thank you for sacrificing your time for me and for our kids. Though they don't always want to be held captive to a "car sermon," how thankful I am that our children have a father who doesn't just preach the Word to a congregation, but teaches and applies the Word to their hearts every day.

To my children, Rebecca, David, and Jonathan, you have shaped me to be who I am more than you know. As your mother I have discovered the true joy in giving, as I would do anything for each of you. When you are happy, I'm happy. When you are sad, I'm sad. But as you grow older I am confronted with the reality that I can no longer just stick a Band-Aid on and make everything better. No, life and your hearts require something so much deeper. The best thing I can do for you is point you to the One who can and does make all things new. The One who gives true joy, peace, and rest. I pray that he is the treasure that you seek all the days of your life.

And thank you to my parents, Sheryl and Doug Bech, and my in-laws, Jean and Chris Hatton, who are living examples of what it means to die to self and live for another. You have been married for almost or in excess of your golden anniversary—wow! What a blessing to have this heritage of faithfulness in marriages, a testimony to God's grace. Your love of the Father, commitment to each other, and continual love for us, your family, is the greatest gift you could ever hand down.

I have also been blessed with many true friends, both near and far. You have prayed for and supported me on this new journey of writing, and it has not gone unnoticed. I appreciate your encouragement via text, e-mail, and phone calls during the somewhat isolating season of writing. Knowing that you cared about me and wanted to see this succeed helped keep me motivated.

A special thank-you to Jeannine McMeans and Cheryl Devoe for your editing help. Jeannine, you went above and beyond by reading and editing along the way in the midst of your own busy life. You were always gracious, encouraging, and honest in your critique—just what I needed to craft each week's devotionals. Furthermore, it is blessing to know I can always turn to you as my friend who has gone before me in the world of parenting teens. And Cheryl, clearly I was in need of your editing expertise. I greatly benefited by your instruction on proper uses of punctuation and pronouns, among other things, that have been long forgotten since high school English! Your set of eyes as a trusted and skilled friend gave me the reassurance I needed before sending the manuscript off.

I am also grateful for my publisher, New Growth Press—especially Cheryl White and Barbara Juliani—for seeing the value of this book and believing in me to complete it. My providential introduction to Cheryl was so clearly orchestrated by the Author of all things and it was what set my dream for this book in motion.

Thank you to Skip Ryan, Rod Mayes, and Lauren Nelson, for reviewing the manuscript in its earliest form and offering your hearty endorsements. For a first-time author like me, it was a big deal to have your support.

Finally, a big shout-out to the original Bible study girls who along with my daughter faithfully met me each week throughout middle school—Ashley, Ashton, Emily, Emily, Hannah Rose, Lauren, Mary Kate, Morgan, Olivia, Rachel, and Regan. And to those who have joined in regularly during the high school years, attending Saturday morning brunch and study time as your busy schedules allow—Amanda, Amber, Annie, Averi, Avery, Cameron, Elise, Kinsey, Kylee, Lilly, Lindsey, Piper, Rachel, Sarah, and Shea. To all of you and Rebecca, thank you for letting me into your world. I pray your desire to study God's Word will always be a consuming fire never to be put out, and through it you will see and behold Christ, resting in his work in life and in death on your behalf.

Endnotes

1. Meredith G. Kline, *Kingdom Prologue: Genesis Foundations for a Covenantal Worldview* (Eugene: Wipf & Stock Publishers, 2006), 26–27.

2. C. S. Lewis, *Mere Christianity* (New York: Macmillan, 1960), 136.

3. Cornelius Plantinga, Jr., *Engaging God's World: A Christian Vision of Faith, Learning, and Living* (Grand Rapids: Eerdmans, 2002), 20–23.

4. *Merriam-Webster's Collegiate Dictionary.* 11th ed., s.v. "enmity."

5. Noel Chartier, "351 Prophecies Fulfilled in Jesus Christ." *AccordingtotheScriptures.org: Religion & Christianity—Bible & Cults—Jesus Christ.* August 12, 2008, accessed March 3, 2014, http://www.accordingtothescriptures.org/prophecy/353prophecies.html.

6. Sam McBratney, *Guess How Much I Love You* (Somerville: Candlewick Press, 1996).

7. Jeffrey C. Hatton, sermon entitled "Walk by the Spirit," Redeemer Presbyterian, Waco, Texas, February 13, 2011, *Redeemerwaco.org*, accessed March 3, 2014, http://redeemerwaco.org/media.php?pageID=6.

8. Paul David Tripp, *Instruments in the Redeemer's Hands: People in Need of Change Helping People in Need of Change* (Phillipsburg, NJ: P&R Publishing, 2002), 85–86.

9. *Merriam-Webster's Collegiate Dictionary.* 11th ed., s.v. "abide.